Criminal Warrants

Scottish Criminal Law and Practice Series

Series Editor

The Rt Hon The Lord McCluskey

Criminal Warrants

Charles N Stoddart LLB, LLM (McGill), PhD, SSC
Sheriff of North Strathclyde at Paisley

Edinburgh
Butterworths
1991

United Kingdom	Butterworth & Co (Publishers) Ltd, 4 Hill Street, EDINBURGH EH2 3JZ and 88 Kingsway, LONDON WC2B 6AB
Australia	Butterworths Pty Ltd, SYDNEY, MELBOURNE, BRISBANE, ADELAIDE, PERTH, CANBERRA and HOBART
Canada	Butterworths Canada Ltd, TORONTO and VANCOUVER
Ireland	Butterworths (Ireland) Ltd, DUBLIN
Malaysia	Malayan Law Journal Sdn Bhd, KUALA LUMPUR
New Zealand	Butterworths of New Zealand Ltd, WELLINGTON and AUCKLAND
Puerto Rico	Equity de Puerto Rico, Inc, HATO REY
Singapore	Butterworth & Co (Asia) Pte Ltd, SINGAPORE
USA	Butterworth Legal Publishers, ST PAUL, Minnesota, SEATTLE, Washington, BOSTON, Massachusetts, AUSTIN, Texas and D & S Publishers, CLEARWATER, Florida

A CIP Catalogue record for this book is available from the British Library.

ISBN 0 406 10582 0

Typeset by Type Aligne, Edinburgh
Printed and bound by Thomson Litho Ltd, East Kilbride, Scotland

Preface

The subject of criminal warrants is mentioned in all the published work on Scottish criminal procedure, but it has never been given the prominence that it deserves. So varied are the circumstances in which warrants may be craved and so commonly are they issued that the absence of a work solely devoted to the topic is somewhat surprising. This book is an attempt to fill that gap. Although the material included herein is largely concerned with police powers, the wider aspects of that topic are not covered, nor are the general issues of civil liberties and human rights explored in any more detail than that absolutely necessary for a proper exposition of the law of warrants.

It is hoped that this book will be of use primarily to practitioners, particularly those faced with urgent decisions on whether warrants are necessary for particular aspects of the criminal process. Included in this category of reader are the professional judiciary and lay magistracy upon whom the task of considering applications for warrants of all kinds is a regular part of their duties. The book will also be of interest to the police and in the universities, particularly for those students involved in the Diploma in Legal Practice at the Scottish universities.

I am grateful to my publishers for including this volume in their excellent series 'Scottish Criminal Law and Practice' and to The Right Honourable The Lord McCluskey, the series editor, for his most useful comments and encouragement. Special thanks are also due to Sheriff PGB McNeill, Sheriff of Lothian and Borders at Edinburgh and to Mr John Macdonald, Assistant Procurator Fiscal at Paisley, for allowing me to draw upon their respective collections of styles in preparing the Appendix. Miss Elizabeth McCallum of the Department of Professional Practice at the Faculty of Law at Strathclyde University has almost single-handedly converted the manuscript into an acceptable form. I am indebted to her for her forbearance.

My wife and daughter have once again had to endure many hours without my company. That they have both remained cheerful and supportive is a matter of great comfort.

The law is stated as at 31 May, 1991.

Charles N Stoddart
Glasgow 14 July, 1991

Contents

Table of statutes

Table of cases

Abbreviations

Case Reports

AC	Law Reports, Appeal Cases (House of Lords and Privy Council) 1890–
Adam	Adam's Justiciary Reports 1894 – 1919
All ER	All England Law Reports 1936 –
CMLR	Common Market Law Reports 1962 –
EHRR	European Human Rights Reports 1979 –
Irv	Irvine's Justiciary Reports 1851 – 68
JC	Justiciary Cases 1917 –
JCL	Journal of Criminal Law
JR	Juridical Review 1889 –
M	Macpherson's Session Cases 1862 – 73
R(J)	Justiciary Cases in Rettie's Session Cases 1873 – 98
SC	Session Cases 1907 – ; Supreme Court
SCCR	Scottish Criminal Case Reports 1981 –
SLT	Scots Law Times 1909 –
White	White's Justiciary Reports 1885 – 93
WLR	Weekly Law Reports (England) 1953 –

Textbooks

Alison *Practice*: Archibald Alison *Practice of the Criminal Law of Scotland* (1833)

Hume: David Hume *Commentaries on the Law of Scotland Respecting Crimes* (1844 edn, by B R Bell)

Renton & Brown: R W Renton and H H Brown *Criminal Procedure according to the Law of Scotland* (5th edn, 1983, by G H Gordon)

Sheehan: A V Sheehan *Criminal Procedure* (1990)

1. General aspects

INTRODUCTION

Definition

1.01 A criminal warrant may be defined as an order by a judge exercising criminal jurisdiction that an individual (or individuals) authorised by law to execute a deliverance of the court shall put it into effect. The warrant may be intended to achieve many different purposes, such as the apprehension of an offender, search of premises or committal to prison. Warrants may also be granted whereby authority is given to carry out executive acts, such as to cite witnesses for precognition or to convene a special sitting of court. But all warrants have the same essential feature: they are the means by which other persons carry out the order of the judge; whatever may have been the position in former times, nowadays the court itself does not act personally but only through the medium of its proper officers and those authorised to act on its behalf.

Historical background

1.02 The granting of a warrant to carry out the order of a judge exercising criminal jurisdiction is a process as old as that jurisdiction itself. From early times it was recognised that those judicial officers empowered to administer the criminal law were entitled to invoke the support of others in carrying into effect orders made under their competent authority. This process long predates both the emergence of organised criminal courts as we know them today and the formation of centralised police forces whose officers now execute warrants as a daily incident of their working lives.[1] In very early times, the authority of the judge was transmitted verbally; the Sheriff might invoke the assistance of his officer, local landowners or the public at large in efforts to arrest fugitives and criminals. Many early statutes were passed requiring that such assistance be given, and penalties were imposed in cases of refusal.[1]

In the seventeenth century parish constables established by statute were given certain powers of arrest which might be reinforced by warrant from a justice of the peace.[2] But it was only later, with the movement away from a localised criminal jurisdiction to a situation where each of a small number of judges presided over a larger geographical area, that the problem of enforcement required to be properly addressed. The emergence of municipal police forces facilitated this process; the police acquired the general duty of enforcing criminal warrants which had hitherto depended largely on the public's sense of civic responsibility, loyalty to the local nobleman or fear of the consequences of non-co-operation.[3]

Increased jurisdiction inevitably carried with it an increase in the range of competent orders which might require to be put into effect by warrant. This was well recognised by 1800, the year when Hume first published his *Commentaries on the Law of Scotland Respecting Crimes*, being the procedural accompaniment to his work on *Description of Crimes*, published three years earlier. Both Hume and Alison, whose later works *Principles of the Criminal Law of Scotland* (1832) and *Practice of the Criminal Law in Scotland* (1833) also became standard texts, cite a number of examples of the exercise of the power to grant warrants and provide a valuable insight into the practice of the time as to apprehension and precognition.[4] It has to be remembered that the High Court of Justiciary had become established only in 1672, that heritable jurisdictions had been abolished as late as 1748 and that the importance of the burgh court had been decreasing as the sheriff acquired greater powers. The cases referred to by Hume and Alison refer to warrants being granted by sheriffs, magistrates and justices of the peace, all of whom had different criminal jurisdiction throughout the centuries as the importance of their respective offices changed.[5]

Hume's treatment of criminal warrants is exclusively (and not surprisingly) confined to the subjects of apprehension and search. By contrast with today, little statutory law on the subject existed in the eighteenth and nineteenth centuries, but this was later to change dramatically. As the commission of crime became more widespread and as new statutory offences were created, the necessity of warrants for enforcement became even more evident. Nowadays there is a deep overlay of statute upon a common law base.[6] But apprehension and search (in both its traditional and modern senses) remain the principal activities for which present-day warrants require to be issued.

1   For an account of the procedures for apprehension in early times, see J Irvine Smith

'Criminal Procedure' in *An Introduction to Scottish Legal History* (Stair Soc vol 20, 1958) p 426 ff.
2 See eg Acts 1617 (c 8) and 1661 (c 38).
3 Glasgow and Edinburgh both obtained private Acts of Parliament at the start of the nineteenth century to enable them to establish their own organised police forces; many other Scottish towns soon followed.
4 Hume II, ch 2; Alison *Practice*, ch 5.
5 For the history of the Scottish criminal courts, see Sheehan *Criminal Procedure* para 1-04 ff, and references there cited.
6 For the whole subject of statutory search warrants, see *infra* para 4.01ff.

WHO MAY APPLY FOR A WARRANT?

1.03 Before the right to prosecute in the public interest became vested in the Lord Advocate and before the procurator fiscal acquired the status in the criminal justice system which he enjoys today, the concept of 'applying' for a warrant was hardly recognised. Jurisdiction was local, irregularly exercised and open to many abuses. In appropriate cases, the authority of the judge was given, rather than sought.[1] Nowadays, the position is reversed; the power to seek warrants is usually exercised by the Crown as a preliminary to or incident of prosecution on behalf of the state. Exceptionally, warrants may be sought by other persons or organisations authorised by statute to prosecute,[2] or where a private individual is granted criminal letters by the High Court.[3] Normally, warrants are sought by the Fiscal, either at common law or under statute. In addition, some statutes themselves give power to particular individuals exercising an investigatory function under the statute to seek a warrant for the enforcement of the prohibition. For example, officers of HM Customs and Excise and of the Department of Trade and Industry enjoy quite extensive powers in this regard;[4] these are examined later.[5] In the usual case however, if the police in the exercise of their duties wish to search particular premises or present a case to the Fiscal justifying the issue of an apprehension warrant, it is the Fiscal who will prepare the necessary application to the appropriate magistrate. Likewise, if more particular warrants are necessary, applications proceed at the instance of the Crown.

1 See *supra* para 1.01.
2 See *Renton and Brown* para 13-13 ff. For example, under the Education (Scotland) Act 1962, s 43 proceedings may be taken either by the public prosecutor or someone authorised by the education authority to act on its behalf.
3 In *X* v *Sweeney* 1982 SCCR 161 criminal letters were issued for a private prosecution for rape. Warrants were issued for apprehension: see 1982 SCCR 161 at 178/179.

4   See eg Value Added Tax Act 1983, s 38 and Sch 7; Wireless Telegraphy Act 1949,
    s 15; *Oldfield*, Complainer 1988 SLT 734.
5   See *infra* paras 4.06–4.08, 4.46–4.48, 4.53–4.55

METHOD OF APPLICATION: PROCEDURAL SPECIALITIES

Standard style of application and warrant

1.04   Certain warrants may be applied for orally. It is a common-place in summary criminal proceedings for a warrant to apprehend an accused person who has failed to attend for trial to be granted under s 338(1) of the Criminal Procedure (Scotland) Act 1975 (the '1975 Act') following oral application by the procurator fiscal at the bar of the court. Similar considerations apply to a warrant to apprehend a witness for failure to attend, all in terms of s 320 thereof. Apart from such cases however, the necessity of specifying the basis in fact and in law for the application renders essential its presentation in writing.

A written application for a warrant is generally regarded as an 'incidental application' under s 310 of the 1975 Act which provides that where prior to or after the presentation of a complaint it is necessary to apply to a court for any warrant or order of court as incidental to proceedings by complaint, or where a court has power to grant any warrant or order of court, although no subsequent proceedings by complaint may follow thereon, such application may be by petition at the instance of a prosecutor in the form set out in Part I of Schedule 2 to the Summary Jurisdiction (Scotland) Act 1954 (or in an Act of Adjournal under the 1975 Act) or as nearly as may be in such form, and where necessary for the execution of any such warrant or order of court, warrant to break open lockfast places shall be implied.

The statutory style of petition contains a heading setting out the name of the statute or statutes under which it is presented and the court to which the petition is addressed. The name of the petitioner, along with his designation is then stated, along with averments as to the factual circumstances and the statutory provisions, if any, on which the application is based. Lastly, there is a crave setting out the warrant desired by the petitioner. The standard form of warrant, which is adaptable as the circumstances require, is in the following terms :

'The court having considered the foregoing petition grants warrant as craved.'[1]

> [*signature*]
> Sheriff

If by statute the warrant can only be granted after sworn information is presented by or on behalf of the applicant, then the following styles are in common use:

At   the   day of   19 .
In the presence of [*name*]
Sheriff of [*name of court*]
COMPEARED the said [*name of deponent*] who being solemnly sworn and examined, depones that what is contained in the foregoing Petition is true as he shall answer to God

> [*signatures*]
> Deponent
> Sheriff

At   the   day of   19 .

The Sheriff having considered the foregoing Petition and relative Oath, grants warrant to (*carry out acts authorised*) as craved.

> [*signature*]
> Sheriff

There is to be found in the Appendix a collection of detailed styles of those Applications for warrants commonly encountered in practice.[2]

---

1 For a detailed examination of the formalities of a warrant, see *infra* paras 1.10–1.17.
2 See *infra* p 122 ff.

Service and intimation of application

1.05   On the lodging of the application for a warrant, one matter which requires to be considered is whether it should be served on the person who may be affected by the acts sought to be authorised, or whether there is anyone having an interest to whom the application ought to be intimated. The position varies depending upon the type of application. In many cases involving warrants to search premises, it would be fatuous to insist on service of the application upon the householder before consideration of the application, for vital evidence which might be recovered, such as stolen property, might disappear in the interim period. In such cases the law imposes on the sheriff or magistrate the duty of ensuring that the application is properly presented and considered, having regard not just to the public interest, but also to the private rights of the individual.

As it was put by Lord Justice-General Clyde in the context of a case concerning a warrant to take dental impressions of a suspect:

'Although the accused is not present or legally represented at the hearing where the magistrate grants the warrant to examine or to search, the interposition of an independent judicial officer affords the basis for a fair reconciliation of the interests of the public in the suppressions of crime and of the individual, who is entitled not to have the liberty of his person or his premises unduly jeopardised.'[1]

It is submitted that these *dicta* are apt to cover many cases of search and apprehension, whether at common law or statute. But there are cases where either statute expressly provides for service and/or intimation, or the wider interests of justice may require it. For example, an application under the provision of s 7 of the Bankers' Books Evidence Act 1879 for an order for inspection of a banker's books may be made 'with or without summoning the bank or any other party', which clearly implies that a court may hear argument on behalf of the bank before an order is made, and for that purpose may order service of the application.[2]

Likewise, where an accused person has been fully committed under solemn procedure and it is subsequently decided to apply for a warrant (eg to take his fingerprints or search his person) then the application should be served on the accused so that the court considering it can hear a proper contradictor to the arguments in support of the application. This procedure was followed in *HM Advocate v Milford*[3] (warrant to take a blood sample); *Lees v Weston*[4] (fingerprints) and *McGlennan v Kelly*[5] (hair sample).

Accordingly it would seem appropriate for the court in all cases to consider whether service is necessary or whether the interests of the person concerned can be adequately safeguarded by virtue of the exercise of the judicial function. It is thought that on principle a decision to order service would be open to appeal by the applicant, but there are no reported cases on the point.

1 *Hay v HM Advocate* 1968 JC 40 at 46.
2 On the details of the 1879 Act, see *infra* paras 4.03–4.05.
3 1973 SLT 12.
4 1989 SLT 446.
5 1989 SCCR 352, 1989 SLT 832.

Consideration of the application

1.06 An application presented to a magistrate or other judge is usually considered in private, unless because of the necessity of hearing full argument for both sides it is appropriate to consider the matter in open court. It is within the power of the judge to hear argument in support of the application, either from the applicant himself or, in cases where he thinks it necessary[1] or where statute requires,[2] by taking the oath of an appropriate investigative officer (eg a detective constable) as to the factual basis of the application and by considering in that light its legal justification. Applications are always dealt with simply on the basis of *ex parte* statements; proof in the traditional sense, tested in cross examination, is of course entirely inappropriate.

1 See *Hume* II, 77; Alison, *Practice* 121.
2 For example, Firearms Act 1968, s 46; Misuse of Drugs Act 1971, s 23(3).

The granting of the warrant

1.07 If satisfied that the application is well founded both in point of form and on its merits, a written warrant is signed and issued to the person(s) authorised to execute it. In summary cases, execution upon any warrant may proceed either upon such warrant itself or upon an extract thereof issued and signed by the clerk of court.[1] The warrant can then be put into execution in the manner and for the purposes expressly authorised.[2]

In summary cases, on a complaint under the 1975 Act being laid before the court, the judge has power under s 314(1) to grant all competent warrants; frequently he will be asked to grant an initiating warrant for the apprehension of the accused and search of his person, dwelling house and repositories 'and any place where he may be found for any documents, articles or property likely to afford evidence of his guilt of, or guilty participation in, any offence charged in the complaint, and to take possession of such documents, articles or property.' By s 314(2), power to grant an apprehension warrant under that section is exercisable notwithstanding that there is power, whether at common law or under any Act to apprehend him without a warrant.[3]

1   1975 Act, s 309(2).
2   On the question of irregular searches and their evidential consequences, see *infra* para 5.05ff.
3   On the whole subject of apprehension warrants, see *infra* paras 2.01–2.10.

WHO MAY GRANT A WARRANT?

Common law and statutory warrants: general considerations

1.08   A common law warrant may be granted by any judge and his power to do so is only limited by the territorial jurisdiction which he exercises. Accordingly, judges of the High Court can grant any warrant at common law for execution anywhere in Scotland, while sheriffs and justices of the peace enjoy a jurisdiction limited in the first instance by their sheriffdom and commission area respectively.[1]

By contrast, a warrant issued under statute can, it is submitted, only be granted by the particular judge mentioned in the statute. A more senior judicial officer cannot exercise the powers of someone more junior in the hierarchy if the statute confers jurisdiction only on the latter. The point arose sharply in the case of a warrant granted under the Official Secrets Act 1911 to search the premises of the BBC in 1987. A sheriff granted the warrant, even although the statute empowered only a justice of the peace to do so. This was later justified on the basis that the sheriff was said to be exercising a common law jurisdiction, something which flew in the face of the application for the warrant, which was made under the statute.[2]

1   For an examination of the position where it is sought to execute a warrant outwith the territorial jurisdiction of the granter, see *infra* paras 1.09, 1.19.
2   See the correspondence *sub nom* 'JP's, Sheriffs and Official Secrets' (1987) 32 JLSS 138, 222, 253. *MacNeill*, Complainer, 1983 SCCR 450 deals with a different point: the common law right of the Crown to seek a search warrant prior to charge for either common law or statutory offences. It does not address the issue of which judge may grant a warrant sought in terms of a statute.

Search warrants

1.09 A search warrant relates of course to the search of premises at a particular locality. But one question which arises frequently in practice is which judge is entitled to grant such a warrant? Is it the judge having jurisdiction over the crime which is alleged to have been committed, or the judge in the jurisdiction where it is proposed to carry out the search? The problem is not addressed by the institutional writers and has led to a considerable divergence of judicial view.[1] It is submitted that the proper course is for the judge who has jurisdiction over the *locus* of the crime to grant the warrant, even if the premises to be searched are outwith his jurisdiction, subject to the concurrence of a judge having jurisdiction there. In these circumstances a crave for warrant of concurrence is added to the application, and such a warrant is added by the concurring judge when the original search warrant is put before him.[2]

1 Both Hume and Alison refer only to warrants of apprehension when discussing the territory within which a warrant may be granted: see *Hume* II, 77; *Alison* Practice, 123, 125.
2 This is the practice in many parts of Scotland, although one alternative is for the procurator fiscal for the district in which the crime was committed to forward the papers to his colleague in the district where the search is proposed so that a search warrant may be obtained locally. This method is rather more cumbersome and time-consuming than the suggested procedure.

FORMALITIES OF A WARRANT

Introduction

1.10 There is now a considerable body of law on the question of formal validity of a warrant. Increased public awareness of individual rights coupled with the need to provide adequate protection for those who execute the orders of a court has led to greater concentration on the wording of an application for a warrant and on the terms in which the warrant itself is expressed. The law requires certain minimum standards of formality before a warrant becomes *ex facie* valid; other particulars are desirable as a matter of good practice, but their absence may not have the effect of rendering ineffective the actings done under the warrant or of excluding as inadmissible in a later trial the evidence of those actings or their results.[1]

Before the requirements are considered in detail, it should be observed that an *ex facie* valid warrant is effective and will stand until it is suspended or reduced; in particular, a court cannot go behind its terms and explore the issue whether the warrant ought to have been granted in the first place.[2] But a warrant which is *ex facie* invalid is bad; procedure following thereon is inept. It is for this reason that great care should be taken in preparing both the application for a warrant and the warrant itself; as will be seen, both are often contained within the same document; the warrant frequently refers back to the earlier crave.[3]

1 On the whole issue of the powers of a trial court when dealing with a search warrant which is challenged and with the admissibility of evidence of actings done thereunder, see *infra* para 5.01ff.
2 *Allan v Tant* 1986 SCCR 175. On suspension of a warrant, see *infra* para 1.26.
3 On the basic style of warrant see *supra* para 1.04.

Is a written warrant necessary?

1.11 In modern practice all warrants issued by a competent court are in written form. But Hume states that any magistrate who has knowledge of a serious crime, or a riot or breach of the peace may authorise by way of verbal order the apprehension of the offender, whether he has witnessed the crime himself, or received an immediate complaint of its commission.[1] But he says that this course of action will only be justified in urgent cases, where there is a risk that the person will escape through the delay of waiting for a written warrant.[1] There are no recent reported examples of the exercise of this right, no doubt because of the existence of an organised and mobile police force with good communications. In addition, there are extensive common law and statutory powers of the police to arrest without warrant.[2]

1 Hume II, 75.
2 See *Renton and Brown*, para 5-18 ff.

Subscription

1.12 Hume and Alison concur in stating that warrants to apprehend and to search must be subscribed personally by the magistrate who grants them.[1] This is in accordance with the general requirement of Scots law that all important documents be authenticated in this manner; it can thus be safely inferred that all other types of warrant likewise require subscription. Only the Sovereign may superscribe deeds, but no modern warrants are granted personally by the Head of State. Many statutes provide for the 'issue' or 'grant' of a warrant, which provisions are usually interpreted as requiring subscription; and summary warrants of apprehension and search 'shall be signed by the judge granting the same ...'[2] In *HM Advocate v Bell*[3] a warrant under s 23(3) of the Misuse of Drugs Act 1971 was held to be invalid where it was not signed, although the name of the magistrate granting it had been written by her in the body of the warrant; the absence of any subscription at all was fatal.

But there may be some small doubt that the requirement of signature extends to personal manuscript signature. In *Cardle v Wilkinson*[4] it was held that a document (in that case DVLC print-out) might be authenticated by a person affixing to it a rubber stamp facsimile of his signature, all in the context of a particular statute which referred to a document 'purporting to be' authenticated by an authorised person. In the commentary on the decision it is suggested that where the law requires an actual and not merely a purported signature, a rubber stamp will still suffice, but it will have to be proved that it was the signature of the purported signatory and was affixed by (or at least with the authority of) the purported signatory.[5] This view remains to be tested in the context of the law of warrants; it sits uneasily alongside institutional authority that the handwriting of the granter is required. In any event, it is thought that neither applicants for warrants nor granters thereof are likely to take the risks inherent in anything other than manuscript signature. Likewise, apprehension or search warrants, cannot be signed on behalf of the judge by his clerk or another official.

The situation is slightly different in those exceptional cases where a warrant may be granted by the Secretary of State. Both the Interception of Communications Act 1985 and the Security Service Act 1989 allow the Secretary of State to 'issue' a warrant for certain purposes. Detailed discussion of these statutes is reserved until later,[6] but under s 4(1) of the 1985 Act it is specifically provided that a warrant shall not be issued except (a) under the hand of the Secretary of State; or (b) in an urgent case where the Secretary of State has expressly authorised its issue and a statement of that fact is endorsed thereon, under the hand of an official of his department of or above the rank of Assistant Under Secretary of State. Section 3(3) of the 1989 Act makes similar provision, except that in urgent cases, the issue of the warrant may be under the hand of an official of or above Grade 3 in the civil service hierarchy.[7]

1   *Hume* II, 78; Alison *Practice*, 122, 146.
2   1975 Act, s 309(2).

3   1984 SCCR 430.
4   1982 SCCR 33.
5   Ibid p 38.
6   See *infra* paras 4.57–4.61.
7   Both of these statutes make specific provision for signature; but see *HM Advocate v Copeland* 1987 SCCR 232 on the question of the issue of a direction (not a warrant) for extended detention under the Prevention of Terrorism (Temporary Provisions) Act 1984.

The office held by the granter

1.13   Hume says that a warrant (to arrest) must be under the hand 'of the magistrate in whose name it runs'.[1] He goes on to suggest that a warrant, if granted by a justice of the peace, ought regularly to bear his 'style and quality', and the 'county for which, as well as the place where, it is given'; but concludes that there is no ground for suggesting that the want of such particulars, apart from 'subscription of the magistrate' renders the warrant void.[1] Hume's view is echoed by Alison,[2] and is reflected in the fact that the style of warrant presently prescribed by statute contains no designation for the granter.[3] This is surprising in an age when large numbers of warrants are granted annually by sheriffs and magistrates whose identities (at least in urban communities) are unlikely to be known to the public at large, as opposed to those persons who attend court regularly in whatever capacity. The sheriff and the baillie may not, in the late eighteenth and nineteenth centuries, have suffered from any problems of anonymity in the communities in which they served and their authority would probably have been recognised without difficulty and acted upon without recourse to a formality which doubtless to them would have seemed otiose. In modern times, when crime is widespread, criminals more sophisticated and the holders of judicial office more numerous, the complete absence in a warrant (either *in gremio* or by reference back to the earlier application) of any designation or statement identifying the granter ought, it is submitted, to be fatal. It has to be said, however, that this was not the view taken by the sheriff in *HM Advocate v Strachan*[4], in which the omission of the sheriff's name and designation in a drugs warrant was held not to render the warrant invalid. The sheriff founded on *Alison* and was not swayed by an unreported decision of Lord Dunpark in *HM Advocate v Bray*[5], where, apparently, the opposite view was taken. Until the matter is authoritatively settled by the High Court sitting as an appeal court, the law would appear to be somewhat uncertain, but it is suggested that modern Scots law requires (or should require) that a written warrant, whether for arrest or for other purposes, must bear on its face to have been granted by a competent official, either by designing him *in gremio* of the warrant or by the addition of his designation to his signature so that any person executing the warrant (who may be liable to civil action for wrongful invasion of liberty) and any person who is the subject of the actings authorised by the warrant (who is thus to have his liberty invaded) can be instantly aware of the authority under which the warrant is granted.

1   *Hume* II, 78.
2   Alison *Practice* p 123.
3   1975 Act, s 310, referring to the form in Pt I of Sch 2 to the Summary Jurisdiction (Scotland) Act 1954.
4   1990 SCCR 341.
5   High Court, Aberdeen, February 1990, unreported.

Actings authorised by the warrant

1.14   It is clear that a wide and indefinite warrant is illegal, whether that is to apprehend all persons suspected of a crime, or search all premises for the proceeds of a theft.[1] In relation to search warrants, particular premises must always be specified with details of what articles the search is authorised to locate. This matter is discussed more fully later.[2] Likewise, if the warrant proceeds under statute rather than common law, that fact should be made clear. The practical importance of these requirements in relation to search warrants cannot be overstressed, for frequently an argument is advanced at the subsequent trial of the offender that the terms of the warrant were exceeded, because articles were recovered other than those for which a search was authorised.[3]

1   Hume II, 78; Alison *Practice*, 146, 147; *Nelson v Black & Morrison* (1866) 4 M 328; *Webster v Bethune* (1857) 2 Irv 597.
2   See *infra* paras 3.12, 3.13.
3   See eg *Guthrie v Hamilton* 1988 SCCR 330, 1988 SLT 823. The whole question of the admissibility of evidence obtained beyond the terms of a warrant is considered *infra* para 5.01ff. See also *HM Advocate v McGrade and Stirton* 1982 SLT (Sh Ct) 13.

Persons entitled to execute warrant

1.15   A common law warrant may be addressed to a particular police officer or generally to officers of law under the jurisdiction of the granter. If necessary for the execution of a summary warrant of apprehension and search, officers of law may break open shut and lockfast places;[1] in all cases the officer executing the warrant must acquaint the party with the substance of the warrant by showing it to him,[2] and he must not break open doors until he has been refused admittance.[3]

Particular statutes may require that only a named officer has the authority to proceed. In *HM Advocate v Cumming*, a warrant under s 23(3) of the Misuse of Drugs Act 1971 was challenged *inter alia* on the basis that it did not include the name of, or reference to any constable at all; this was held to be a clear breach of s 23(3), a fatal irregularity which could not be excused.[4] But in *HM Advocate v Bell*, the standard Strathclyde Police drugs warrant came under scrutiny; it provided for warrant to 'any constable of the Strathclyde Police' to carry out the appropriate search. This was not challenged, although the warrant was criticised on other grounds.[5] In drugs and many other cases, this has become the common formula, but in each statutory warrant, the statute itself should be checked to see whether any similar general authority is appropriate.

1   1975 Act, s 321(1).
2   *Hume* II, 79; Alison *Practice*, 124.
3   *Hume* II, 80; Alison *Practice*, 124.
4   1983 SCCR 15.
5   1984 SCCR 430.

Must a warrant be dated?

1.16 Hume states that a warrant to apprehend *ought* to be dated, but goes on to suggest that an undated warrant will not be invalid.[1] He does not deal at all with this requirement in the context of search or other warrants. Alison is of the view that an apprehension warrant *must* be dated, but later qualifies this by agreeing with Hume that absence of a date does not render the warrant void.[2] So far as search warrants are concerned, Alison states that a date is essential.[3] But whatever was the effect of these views in the past, in modern practice all warrants bear the date on which they are granted and, at least in the particular case of search warrants authorising a search within a particular time limit, the absence of a date is fatal. In *Bulloch v HM Advocate*[4] purported warrants under s 37(3) of the Finance Act 1972 to enter and search premises in relation to a VAT offence were held to be invalid. The warrants were dated 'September 1976' with no more precise specification, but authorised searches within fourteen days of their issue. Lord Ross observed that the failure to state the exact date of granting meant that no-one could know whether the warrant was executed within the time limit. He continued:

'Moreover, persons to whom the warrants were exhibited would be unable to determine whether or not the search purported to be made thereunder was valid. As it stands these warrants are defective and I do not consider that the defects can be cured after the warrant has been used and has purported to be put into effect. I know of no authority for the proposition that the lack of a precise date upon a warrant can be made good after the event in a case where the date is critical to the question of validity. It is the sheriff who must certify the date upon which he grants the warrant and where that has not been done I do not consider that evidence from other sources should be admitted to make good the deficiency.'[4]

Accordingly, it is incompetent to lead parole evidence as to when the warrant was signed if the date thereon is missing or incomplete.[5] In *Tudhope v Senatti Holdings Ltd.*,[6] where a warrant assigning a diet in a summary case was undated, the sheriff refused to hold a preliminary proof as to its date, observing that such a procedure would be so unusual and undesirable as to be contrary to public policy.[7] The date on a warrant need not however be located in the body of the warrant itself, provided it appears at some other place directly referable to it, such as after the signature of the granter, and not just in the body of the information which precedes the warrant.[8]

1 *Hume* II, 78.
2 Alison *Practice*, 122, 123.
3 Ibid, 146.
4 1980 SLT (Notes) 5.
5 *HM Advocate v Welsh* 1987 SCCR 647.
6 1984 SCCR 251.
7 Ibid, 254.
8 *HM Advocate v Cumming* 1983 SCCR 15.

Time limits on execution

1.17   Normally common law warrants are executed only once; one apprehension or search is all that is permitted. But some statutes seem to envisage that warrants granted thereunder may be executed repeatedly up to a particular time limit. So, for example, s 23(3) of the Misuse of Drugs Act 1971 permits a search 'at any time *or times* within one month of the date of warrant.' There appear to be no reported examples of cases where repeated searches have been challenged on grounds of oppression or abuse of power.[1]

1 As a matter of practice, one police search is likely to have the effect of ensuring that premises are not used again as a receptacle for keeping controlled drugs, at least for the foreseeable future.

WHERE MAY A WARRANT BE EXECUTED?

Warrants to apprehend

1.18   According to Hume, every sheriff, magistrate of a burgh or justice of the peace, may lawfully grant

'a warrant for his bounds, on due information of any crime, though it be one of that degree which he has not cognisance of, to the effect of trial and punishment.'

This jurisdiction arises, he says,

'from the nature of the commission to such magistrates, which gives them a general charge of the conservation of the peace, within their respective bounds; and it is indispensable towards the advancement of justice, in the case of the greater criminals, who would often escape unpunished, if it were not for this local and speedy course of attaching their persons.'[1]

Alison puts the matter more succinctly: warrant to arrest can be granted by a magistrate to officers of law within his jurisdiction, even for an offence which he is not competent to try or punish.[2] Implicit in both such statements is that the territorial jurisdiction enjoyed by the judge granting the warrant fixes the limit beyond which, generally speaking, the warrant cannot be executed. So, a warrant from the High Court is good throughout Scotland, while that of a sheriff or justice of the peace is, in general terms, limited to his sheriffdom or commission area.

1   *Hume* II, 77.
2   Alison *Practice*, 120, 121.

Execution of apprehension warrant outwith jurisdiction

1.19   It follows from the foregoing that if it is proposed to use a warrant outwith the territory for which the granter has jurisdiction, some further legal formality may be required. In early times, all such warrants had to be 'backed', that is, endorsed by a magistrate of competent jurisdiction for the purpose of authorising the execution of it within his territory. Unless a warrant was backed it had no legal effect outwith the bounds of the jurisdiction of the magistrate issuing it.[1]

Such was the general rule, from which it will be apparent that great difficulty would often arise in the case of offenders moving from one jurisdiction to another. Within Scotland, a warrant to apprehend issued by the High Court of Justiciary is, as indicated earlier, valid throughout Scotland without further action being required. But such warrants are usually issued only for persons who fail to appear for trial or sentence in the High Court, or where an appeal against a custodial sentence by an accused on bail is ultimately refused, or where contempt of the High Court is involved. From the early nineteenth century onwards, the position was eased regarding warrants issued by the inferior courts. Nowadays, most apprehension warrants in Scotland are issued by a sheriff, no doubt because of what are now ss 15 and 327 of the 1975 Act which provide that such a warrant against anyone charged with committing an offence within the sheriff's jurisdiction may be executed throughout Scotland without endorsation. Those sections also apply to a person *in meditatione fugae*; warrants granted thereunder are sufficient not only for apprehension but also for conveying and disposing of the offender. Such a warrant may be executed throughout Scotland in like manner as it may be executed within the jurisdiction of the sheriff who granted the warrant.[2]

Apprehension warrants issued by the district court are covered by the provisions of s 326 of the 1975 Act which provides *inter alia* that any warrant under Part II of the Act may without endorsation be served or executed at any place within Scotland by any officer of law, and such service or execution may be proved either by the oath in court of such officer or by production of his written execution.

Where it is necessary to execute the warrant in England, Wales or Northern Ireland this may be done by virtue of two alternative procedures. The first (and much more cumbersome) is to use the provisions of the Indictable Offences Act 1848 which provides that a warrant issued in Scotland by a judge of the High Court, a sheriff, or a justice of the peace, or a warrant under the Summary Jurisdiction (Scotland) Act 1954 may be endorsed by a justice of the peace who has jurisdiction at the place where it is to be executed. Similar provisions exist for the endorsement in Scotland of warrants issued in other parts of the United Kingdom.[3] Since however the Act is rarely invoked in practice it is not proposed to deal with its provisions in any more detail; the alternative procedure usually employed today is to rely on the provisions of s 38 of the Criminal Law Act 1977 which provide that a warrant of apprehension issued in Scotland may be executed within his police area by any English or Welsh constable, and in Northern Ireland by any member of the Royal Ulster Constabulary, whether or not it has been endorsed under the 1848 Act.

Reciprocal provisions apply to warrants issued in other parts of the United Kingdom for execution in Scotland.[4]

Special provision is made in respect of the execution of Scottish warrants in the Republic of Ireland and *vice versa*. The procedure has been described as mid-way between formal extradition procedure and the simple execution of a warrant outwith Scotland.[5] An Irish warrant which is to be executed in Scotland requires to be backed in terms of the Backing of Warrants (Republic of Ireland) Act 1965 which lays down a detailed procedure. Further provision is made by the Act of Adjournal (Consolidation) 1988 which *inter alia* provides the form of endorsement.[6] In addition, the Backing of Warrants (Republic of Ireland) Act 1967 empowers a sheriff or justice of the peace in Scotland to issue a 'provisional warrant' in limited circumstances where a warrant issued in Ireland cannot be immediately produced.[7] Execution of Scottish warrants in Ireland is also covered by the 1965 Act.

Warrants issued in the Isle of Man must be backed for execution in Scotland.[8]

---

1   *Hume* II, 78; Alison *Practice*, 124, 125. Backing was achieved by a certificate attached to the warrant to the effect that the endorsing magistrate was satisfied by proof that the signature on the warrant was that of the purported granter; he thereafter authorised execution in his own jurisdiction.
2   1975 Act, ss 15(2), 327(2).
3   Indictable Offences Act 1848, ss 14, 15.
4   Criminal Law Act 1977, s 38(2). This Act does not apply to warrants emanating from or to be executed in the Channel Islands; in such cases the procedure under the Indictable Offences Act 1848 (as amended by the Indictable Offences Act Amendment Act 1868) must be used. For the execution of warrants by police in the border area of Scotland and England, see Police (Scotland) Act 1967, s 18.
5   Sheehan, *Criminal Procedure*, para 3.10. For a summary of the law, see Renton and Brown, para 5-52. See also *Simpson v McLeod* 1986 SCCR 237.
6   Act of Adjournal (Consolidation) 1988, Rules 148 to 152.
7   Backing of Warrants (Republic of Ireland) Act 1967, ss 2A, 4.
8   1975 Act, ss 16, 324.

Search warrants

1.20   The position where it is sought to execute a search warrant outwith the jurisdiction of the judge who granted it has already been noted.[1]

---

1   See *supra* para 1.09.

Where extradition necessary

1.21 Extradition from Scotland is covered by the provisions of the Extradition Acts 1870 and 1989. Certain warrants and orders may be issued under each statute. Since extradition is rarely encountered in Scottish practice, it has not been thought necessary to deal with the matter in detail here, and the reader is referred to the standard procedural text which sets out the current position.[1]

1 See *Renton and Brown* para 5-45 ff.

CAN FORCE BE USED TO EXECUTE A WARRANT?

Compulsion: general considerations

1.22 At the outset, it should be recognised that a warrant is a method of compulsion. The individual who is liable to any kind of court order, whether civil or criminal, may of course submit to it voluntarily. If, for example, someone is found liable in civil damages for breach of contract, he may accept the judgment, pay the damages and conclude the matter without any need for any means of enforcement at the instance of his opponent. Likewise someone who is told of the existence of an order by a criminal court, for example that his house is to be searched for the proceeds of a housebreaking, may invite the police to enter his home and consent to the search without the necessity of any warrant being executed. Similarly the accused who is convicted and sentenced to imprisonment may choose to walk to the cells without the necessity of handcuffs and the accompaniment of an extract sentence and warrant of detention. It is precisely because such civic responsibility cannot be guaranteed that criminal courts do not usually take the risk that their orders will be obeyed without incident or objection and grant warrants accordingly.

But a warrant can only truly be seen as a *compulsitor* where the existence of the warrant is made known to the person potentially affected by it and he refuses to do or permit what is ordered. If the police obtain a search warrant in respect of premises, go there, demand entrance and show the warrant to the occupier, he may refuse to let them enter. In such a situation the warrant overrides the absence of consent, and the police would be justified in carrying out the acts authorised, including opening lockfast places, breaking down doors and the like, always assuming such acts were covered by the warrant or were done otherwise in accordance with the law.[1] The police would be immune from any civil claim by the occupier, who would require simply to stand by and let the search proceed.[2] Every search warrant and apprehension has the same feature; it must be complied with and, if necessary, will be executed irrespective of the wishes of the individual.

1 See eg Criminal Procedure (Scotland) Act 1975, s 321(1).
2 On search warrants generally, see *infra* para 3.01ff.

1.23 Compulsion of course raises the issue of force. An offender who is subject to an apprehension warrant may well be anxious to avoid arrest by as determined and devious means as possible. Faced with imminent arrest, he may not 'come quietly'. Depending on his strength, determination and a host of other factors, his arrest itself may not be accomplished without considerable violence. In the area of personal search and examination, other difficulties arise, for the term 'search' extends beyond personal search of the clothing of the individual to such disparate activities as taking samples of hair or blood;[1] and in that regard a warrant to take samples could only be executed without consent if the suspect was physically restrained.

The question of force thus requires to be addressed in any examination of the law of warrants, because non-forced compliance, although desirable, is not always possible. Suppose, for example, a sheriff grants a warrant to enable the teeth impressions of a suspect to be taken, for the purposes of trying to match them with bite marks found on a victim. The suspect can submit voluntarily to the process or he can refuse. If he refuses, a number of consequences may follow. It may be decided not to enforce the warrant but to charge the suspect with attempting to pervert the course of justice, a charge which, if proved, might result in a different disposal from that which would follow on charge and conviction of the crime originally suspected.[2] It was precisely because of the similar need to provide an adequate sanction in road traffic cases that Parliament created the offence of failure without reasonable excuse to give a blood or urine sample in the case of an individual who did not comply with the breathalyser procedure.[3] But apart from charging with an alternative offence an individual who refuses to comply with a warrant, it may simply be decided to enforce compliance, in which case the degree of force permissible requires to be identified.

1 For the law on such warrants, see *infra* para 3.02ff.
2 The difficulties in such charges have never been adequately explored. 'A charge of failing to comply with a warrant' is a *non-sequitur*; a warrant is granted precisely because there may be a failure to comply.
3 See now Road Traffic Act 1988, s 7(6) and related sections on failures to supply breath specimens.

Force against the individual

1.24 The question of force against the individual in relation to the execution of a common law warrant to apprehend or to search is hardly mentioned by the institutional writers. Each is clear that in order to carry out a warrant, forced entry to premises is permissible if admittance is refused.[1] According to Alison:

'The principle of the law is that every person is bound to throw open his doors, and make patent all the secret parts of his dwelling or premises, in order to facilitate so important an object as the arrest of a criminal; and therefore any resistance to an officer who legally and temperately discharges that duty implicates the resisters in direct disobedience to the law.'[2]

These propositions are reflected in s 321(1) of the 1975 Act whereby it is provided that any warrant of apprehension or search shall, where it is necessary for its execution, imply warrant to officers of law to break open shut and lockfast places.

But this still leaves open the question of the degree of force which may be used against the person in apprehending him or carrying out a personal search. The case law is almost entirely silent on the point: a good example of such silence is *Hay v HM Advocate*,[3] where a warrant to take dental impressions was granted. In that case there seems to have been almost no discussion of the issue of whether the suspect could have been compelled to comply with the warrant, although it was argued that by attending a dental hospital and submitting to the warrant to have his teeth impressions taken, he underwent a technical assault. The warrant in that case did not authorise the use of force; some concession of the difficulty was made by Lord Justice-Clerk Grant (who presided at the trial) when he recognised that a very special circumstance existed where power was sought 'to convey a person, irrespective of his wishes, from one place to another.'[4] Because Hay was an inmate of an approved school at the material time, this difficulty was lessened because the accused 'had largely ceased to be the legal master of his movements.'[4] This, with respect, does not provide a full answer; someone who is determined not to comply with an order of court may require, in the public interest, to be compelled to do so, and the problem requires to be faced squarely, if only for the protection of those given the obligation to enforce the court order. No doubt Hume and Alison are not to be blamed for any such failures: to them the idea of taking teeth impressions from a murder suspect, or examining by means of medical intervention a suspected drugs courier who may have ingested small packets of cocaine would have seemed unthinkable.

But in spite of the absence of discussion, it is probable that Scots law permits the use of 'reasonable' force in the execution of an apprehension warrant or warrant to search the individual. This would be in keeping with the various police powers to act without warrant contained in s 60 of the Civic Government (Scotland) Act 1982, which specifically provides for the use of reasonable force. In any event any excessive use of force carried out with evil intent would render the officer open to a criminal charge of assault and also open up the question of civil damages. It is of course all a question of fact and of degree; in the event of any challenge being later made to the degree of force used, the whole circumstances would presumably be looked at in the light of the competing interests of the state and the individual.

1   *Hume* II, 80; Alison *Practice*, 118, 124.
2   Alison *Practice*, 125.
3   *Hay v HM Advocate* 1968 JC 40.
4   Ibid p 42. See also *Morris v MacNeill* 1991 SCCR 722.

Forced entry to premises

1.25   Here the law is easier to state. Hume and Alison recognise that forced entry to premises for the purpose of executing a warrant may be justified, but only after the officer has made those inside the premises aware of the purpose of the visit and demanded entrance.[1] The common law aside, many statutes authorise the granting of search warrants which may be executed by force.[2] For the reasons advanced above, it is suggested that only 'reasonable' force is appropriate in carrying out the search.[3]

1   Hume II, 80; Alison *Practice*, 124, 125, 146, 147 where both deal with the issue of force in relation to entering premises for the purposes of apprehension or search for stolen goods.
2   See eg Criminal Procedure (Scotland) Act 1975, s 321(1); Firearms Act 1968, s 46(1); Misuse of Drugs Act 1971, s23(3).
3   *Supra*, para 1.24.

APPEALS AGAINST THE GRANT OR REFUSAL OF A WARRANT

1.26   Since an incidental warrant is not regarded as forming part of a criminal case whether proceeding summarily or on indictment, its issue, at least by a sheriff, magistrate or justice of the peace, may be made the subject of appeal by Bill of Suspension to the High Court.[1]

However, it appears that this remedy is not open in the case of warrants issued by the High Court itself, since High Court proceedings cannot be suspended; only those before inferior courts give rise to the mode of appeal.[2]

But the efficacy of this suspension as a remedy may often be open to question, since many warrants are granted as a matter of urgency and are executed immediately; in such cases there may simply be insufficient time for the person affected to come to the High Court of Justiciary by way of Bill.[3] In practice, therefore, there may be little alternative to compliance with the warrant, without prejudice to a later claim that, for instance, any evidence or articles recovered should not be admitted as evidence in subsequent legal proceedings, or indeed that the acts done in executing the warrant were wrongful and give rise to an action of damages. The whole question of evidence improperly obtained is considered later.[4]

Conversely, refusal to grant a warrant may be brought under appeal in the High Court of Justiciary by way of Bill of Advocation at the instance of the prosecutor.[5] In such cases the first deliverance on the Bill of Advocation usually orders service on the person against whom the application for the warrant was directed, and so both sides may be heard by the High Court.[6]

Legal aid is available both to bring such a Bill of Suspension and to resist a Bill of Advocation.[6]

1   For the procedure in Bills of Suspension, see *Renton and Brown*, para 16-33 ff.
2   It is thought that any warrant issued by the High Court could only be appealed by way of petition to the *nobile officium*. There appear to be no reported cases on this point.
3   It was done in 1987 by the BBC in relation to the police raid on their premises in the 'Zircon affair'. The case is not reported, but see *The Scotsman*, 2nd February, 1987.
4   See *infra* para 5.01ff.
5   For the procedure in Bills of Advocation, see *Renton and Brown* para 16-169 *et seq.*
6   In the case of a Bill of Suspension arising before criminal proceedings have started, such an appeal to the High Court is not an appeal against 'conviction, sentence or acquittal' within the terms of the Criminal Legal Aid (Scotland) Regulations 1987, para 4(1)(f), and is accordingly not covered by s 25 of the Legal Aid (Scotland) Act 1986 which applies only to appeals of these categories. The legal aid implications of this problem are yet to arise in practice. Once proceedings have started, then any suspension of a warrant would, it is thought, be treated as part of those proceedings and be covered by any extant legal aid certificate. As for Bills of Advocation, it is suggested that the same considerations apply.

THE EUROPEAN DIMENSION

1.27   The execution of any warrant, whether it be for apprehension, search or other purposes, is of necessity an invasion of personal liberty. Freedom under the law is the hallmark of a civilized society, something which underpins most of the legal rules forming the subject matter of this book. But the domestic law of Scotland need not be the final repository of such rules, for as in many spheres of law it may be necessary to look outside Scotland from time to time to see the extent to which our law and practice conforms to or conflicts with any wider European norm. The United Kingdom is a signatory to the European Convention on Human Rights, an international convention which sets out certain standards in the whole field of civil liberty and fundamental freedom.[1] These standards are recognised in international law by the adherents to the Convention, which also provides certain mechanisms for their enforcement.[2]

It is quite clear however that the Convention is not part of the municipal law of Scotland; Parliament has not (so far) enacted any provisions which incorporate any of the articles of the Convention into statute law here.[3] Accordingly, a party aggrieved by the granting of a warrant cannot invoke the terms of the Convention as an argument in a Scottish court as to whether the warrant was or was not properly granted or whether the acts done thereunder were contrary to Scots law. Nor can he invoke its terms as an aid to construction of any statute under which a warrant may be granted. The domestic law of Scotland is determinative of such issues.[4]

What may however be open to an aggrieved party is the individual entitlement to bring a petition under Article 25 of the Convention to the European Commission of Human Rights with a view to claiming that the state (ie the United Kingdom) has violated his rights under the Convention. He would face a number of obstacles: he would require to have exhausted his domestic remedies; he would have to present his petition timeously; the Commission may not accept it and may not refer it to the European Court of Human Rights. He may not be able to afford the proceedings or get legal aid. But the remedy in successful cases is an award of financial compensation.[5]

It has to be said that Article 5 of the Convention (the right to liberty and security of person) and Article 8 (the right to respect for private and family life, home and correspondence) are both drafted in such wide terms that it is unlikely that any rule of the domestic law of Scotland infringes them. The respective exceptions in Article 5(1) and 8(2) are notable in this regard. Scots law provides domestic remedies for breaches of these rights and it would, as indicated, be incumbent on an aggrieved party to exhaust his domestic remedy first, a process which could extend for a period long after the wrong complained of.[6]

Nonetheless, in theory at least, it might be argued before the

European Court that some hitherto unimagined breach of personal liberty gives rise to the right of individual petition. So far, no such case has arisen in practice.

1   The European Convention (ECHR) was signed in Rome in 1950, ratified by the UK in 1951 and came into force in 1953. For an examination of the Convention, see Ewing & Finnie, *Civil Liberties in Scotland* (2nd edn) ch 2.
2   ECHR, Article 25 ff.
3   The question of incorporation has been discussed endlessly. For a recent attempt at incorporation, see the European Convention on Human Rights Bill 1984, reprinted in *Ewing & Finnie* op cit p 54/55.
4   *Kaur v Lord Advocate* [1980] 3 CMLR 79; *Moore v Secretary of State for Scotland* 1985 SLT 38.
5   ECHR Article 50.
6   The normal domestic remedy would be a civil action for damages. On appeals against the grant of a warrant see *supra* para 1.26.

2. Warrants for apprehension, citation and committal

WARRANTS FOR APPREHENSION

Introduction

2.01 A warrant to apprehend an individual is an order frequently sought in daily practice, and almost as frequently granted. But the factors which the court must weigh in the balance when considering an application for an apprehension warrant vary according to the status of the individual concerned. Deprivation of liberty is a drastic interference with private rights and will only be justified if good legal grounds exist for the order sought. All warrants to apprehend have one thing in common: they are authority only for the arrest of the individual and for his conveyance to and appearance before a court of competent jurisdiction.[1] Once the individual has appeared, the warrant which was the vehicle for his appearance is spent. Further procedure thereafter depends on the order made by the court; if, for example, the court remands him for some purpose, or imposes a custodial sentence, then that is a fresh order necessitating a new warrant of the appropriate type.

It is probably implicit in all warrants to apprehend that such force may be used as is necessary to restrain the person concerned. Apprehension on a legal warrant always involves restriction of movement and compulsion to attend court, including as an incident thereof the submission to police procedures. Although the issue has hardly been explored in the texts and decided cases it is suggested that only 'reasonable' force may be used; excessive use of force raises the question of civil or other remedies.[2]

---

1 *Hume* II, 80; Alison *Practice*, 129; 1975 Act, s 321(2). In *Lockhart v Stokes* 1981 SLT (Sh Ct) 71, a warrant was granted for the apprehension of a person on bail solely for the purposes of serving an indictment on him. This case is highly exceptional; there are thought to have been no similar cases before or since.
2 On the whole question of the execution of a warrant by force, see *supra* paras 1.22–1.25.

Apprehension of suspects

2.02   Under Scots law the general principle is that a suspect is not obliged to go to a police station 'to assist in police enquiries' unless he is formally detained under the provisions of s 2 of the Criminal Justice (Scotland) Act 1980 or other specific statutory power. Accordingly, at common law a warrant to apprehend a suspect is illegal.[1] This is so whether the proposed apprehension is for the purposes of questioning him, searching him at a police station, requiring him to stand in an identification parade or for other reasons. A suspect may of course voluntarily submit to each of these processes, and in restricted cases he may be searched or examined under the authority of a warrant even if he has not been arrested.[2] But that is as far as it goes. At one time the police in Glasgow used what was known as a 'Betty Alexander' warrant, so named because it had been prepared by a former procurator fiscal in the course of an investigation into the murder of a child Betty Alexander. The warrant proceeded on averments that following the investigation of a crime there were reasonable grounds for believing that a named individual might be able to assist in enquiries and that he should be required to stand in an identification parade; it went on to crave warrant to a named police officer 'with such assistance as he may find necessary' to apprehend the individual, search him (and his house) and place him in an identification parade. Such a warrant, sometimes (disparagingly) known by provincial fiscals as a 'Glasgow warrant' was used in the celebrated case of *HM Advocate v Patrick Connolly Meehan*.[3] A petition craving warrant in the above terms had been granted by the Sheriff-Substitute at Glasgow during the investigation into the murder of Mrs Rachel Ross at Ayr in July 1969, as a result of which Patrick Meehan was apprehended, made to stand in a parade and was identified by the deceased's husband. This identification evidence formed a major plank of the Crown case against Meehan, who was convicted of the murder. Following the granting of a Royal Pardon to Patrick Meehan in 1976, Lord Hunter was appointed to conduct an inquiry into the case; in his Report[4] he examined the circumstances in which the warrant was applied for and granted. He recorded the comment that with the possible exception of the warrant to search Meehan's house, it was at least doubtful whether the Petition or the warrant obtained on the strength of it were in the circumstances competent and that in his view the *ratio* of existing authorities would not support its competency.[5] The warrant was not supported in evidence to Lord Hunter's inquiry by any of the Law Officers, ex-Law Officers, Crown Office officials or procurators fiscal who gave evidence to him, even although it had not been objected to by the defence at Meehan's trial, nor had there been any objection then to the admissibility of the evidence obtained under it. While Lord Hunter did not express a concluded view on the matter, the fact is that such warrants are not now encountered in practice; in any event the powers of search (although not the requirement to take part in an identification parade) can now be exercised by the police under s 2 of the Crimnal Justice (Scotland) Act 1980 in respect of a suspect who is formally detained under that section.

1   *Hume* II, 78; Alison *Practice*, 122, 123.
2   See *infra* paras 3.04, 3.05.
3   Edinburgh High Court, October 1969, unreported.
4   *Report of Inquiry into the whole circumstances of the murder of Mrs Rachel Ross* (1982) HC Paper 444, vol 1, paras 3-144 ff.
5   Ibid, paras 3-149.

Apprehension of accused

General provisions

2.03   A warrant may be issued for the apprehension of an accused person in order to commence proceedings against him.[1] If he is to be charged under solemn procedure, the initiating petition which is presented to the sheriff *inter alia* seeks warrant to search for and apprehend the accused 'and meantime, if necessary, to detain him in a police station or other convenient place and to bring him for examination' in respect of the charge. As Renton and Brown put it, such petitions 'being presented by responsible officials, are assumed to be well founded.'[2] The petition is presented to and signed by a sheriff of the sheriff court district in which the offence is alleged to have been committed.[2] In a situation where the accused has already been arrested without warrant, the initial petition warrant is still signed and has the effect of regularising procedure.[3] If the proceedings are to be conducted summarily, an initiating warrant may be granted under s 314(1) of the 1975 Act on the complaint being laid before a judge of the court in which the complaint is brought, if the prosecutor so moves the court. Such power to grant a warrant is exercised 'where this appears to the judge expedient'; and it is exercisable notwithstanding that there is power whether at common law or under any Act to apprehend the individual without warrant.[4] In practice of course, many accused persons making their first appearance in a summary criminal court have either been arrested without warrant[5] or have been simply cited or bailed on an undertaking to attend.[6]

The form of the summary apprehension warrant on a complaint is in simple terms *viz* 'The court grants warrant to apprehend the said accused'. Implied therein is power to officers of law to break open all shut and lockfast places (where necessary) and also to search for and to apprehend the accused and bring him before the court to answer the charge on which the warrant is granted and meantime to detain him in a police station house, police cell or other convenient place.[7] He must be produced to the court quickly: it is specifically provided that a person apprehended under such a warrant shall wherever practicable be brought before a court competent to deal with the case either by way of trial or by way of remit to another court not later than in the course of the first day after he has been taken into custody, such day not being a Saturday, a Sunday or a court holiday prescribed for that court under s 10 of the Bail Etc (Scotland) Act 1980.[8]

1 *Hume* II, 77; Alison *Practice*, 121; 1975 Act, s 314(1).
2 *Renton and Brown* para 5-08.
3 *Peggie v Clark* (1868) 7 M 89 at 93.
4 1975 Act, s 314(1), (2).
5 Ibid, s 321(4).
6 On warrants to cite, see *infra* paras 2.11–2.18. On bail undertakings, see 1975 Act, s 295.
7 1975 Act, s 321(2).
8 Ibid, s 321(3). Nothing therein prevents an accused being brought before the court on such a day where, in terms of s 10 of the 1980 Act, the court is sitting for the disposal of criminal business: s 321(3), *proviso*.

2.04 An accused person who fails to attend for trial, whether under solemn or summary procedure, may be made the subject of a warrant to apprehend.[1] If he has been bailed for trial, it is one of the standard conditions of bail that he attend all diets in the case; if he fails to do so, without reasonable excuse, he commits an offence[2] and his attendance at court to answer the original charge can be enforced by warrant; at that appearance he will also normally be served with a fresh petition or complaint charging him under the Bail Etc (Scotland) Act 1980.

It frequently also happens that an accused person is bailed on one complaint, then commits a further offence for which he is arrested and remanded in custody pending trial. During the period of remand, his trial diet on the original complaint comes up, but due to ignorance of his position on the part of the Crown, he is not brought to court for trial. In such a case the only way his attendance can be enforced is by the grant of a warrant for his apprehension on the first complaint, thus providing the police with the authority to bring the accused from custody.

1 Under solemn procedure, such a warrant is issued at common law; under summary procedure, the situation is governed by s 338 of the 1975 Act. In each case it must be established that he has been cited to attend, or in a summary case, has had intimation of the diet.
2 Bail Etc (Scotland) Act 1980, s 3(1)(a).

2.05 Hume states that when a person is arrested on a warrant he is entitled to see it so that he knows of what he is accused. Any officer who knows of the existence of a warrant is entitled to detain the person named therein until the warrant is found.[1] In practice this is done every day; police warrant checks on suspected persons frequently disclose a host of pending cases, including those where a means enquiry warrant is outstanding. All warrants should thus be shown to the accused on request, but the officer is not obliged to part company with any warrant; as a matter of law and good practice, he should retain possession of it.[1] In *Stirton v Macphail*[2] it was held that a police officer was acting 'in the execution of his duty' within the meaning of s 41(1) of the Police (Scotland) Act 1967 when he arrested a person on a means enquiry warrant, albeit he did not have the warrant with him and indeed proceeded only upon a hearsay account that the warrant existed.

The existence of a warrant to apprehend need not however mean that an actual arrest requires to be carried out. The procurator fiscal may simply arrange for the accused to be brought to court to answer the warrant; and he may be warned that there is a warrant against him and invited to attend.[3] Such arrangements are often made between the Crown and representatives of the accused, who is usually told to present himself at a named police office at a particular time so that police formalities may be completed prior to a court appearance. If the accused fails to keep to the arrangements, the case is not called in court and the extant warrant will be executed in the usual way.

1 *Hume* II, 79; *Renton and Brown* para 5-27.
2 1983 SLT 34.
3 See *Renton and Brown* para 5-27.

Delay in execution of warrant to apprehend

2.06 A warrant to apprehend should be executed as soon as possible.[1] Delay in the execution of a warrant has the obvious effect that proceedings cannot be brought to a speedy conclusion. Most frequently this occurs in summary cases where an accused fails to appear for trial, an apprehension warrant is granted but the accused disappears and is not traced for some considerable time. Outstanding warrants often come to light when a person is charged with an offence and his antecedents are checked; old cases are thus resuscitated or put to rest at the Crown's discretion.

In relation to statutory offences charged on summary complaint, delay in execution sometimes has an important impact on whether the proceedings can be started in the first place. Unless the statute under which the accused is charged provides otherwise, summary proceedings for statutory contraventions must be commenced within six months after the contravention occurred, and in the case of a continuous contravention within six months after the last date of such contravention.[2] It is provided that for these purposes, proceedings are deemed to be commenced on the date on which a warrant to apprehend or to cite the accused is granted, if such warrant is executed without undue delay.[3] Accordingly the issue sometimes arises as to whether the delay in execution of a warrant is 'undue'; if it is, then the proceedings will be time-barred.

1   *Farquhanson v Whyte* (1886) 1 White 26. See also *Newall v Jessop* 1991 SCCR 388, where a preliminary plea to the competency of the proceedings was made, partly on the basis that a warrant to apprehend the accused was not executed for six months.
2   1975 Act, s 331(1).
3   Ibid, s 331(3).

2.07   It is clear that the delay in execution must not be for any reason for which the prosecutor is responsible. The case law on this subject has developed mainly in relation to non-timeous execution of warrants to cite rather than warrants to apprehend, although the principles are the same. The subject is therefore discussed in more detail later in this text.[1]

1   See *infra* paras 2.13–2.15.

Apprehension of witnesses

2.08   A warrant may be issued for the apprehension of a witness who, having been lawfully cited to attend a criminal trial to give evidence either for the Crown or the Defence fails so to attend or indicates in advance of the trial that he intends to abscond.[1] In cases proceeding under solemn procedure, the warrant is issued at common law, following a petition by either Crown or Defence supported by a statement on oath that the witness has absconded (or means to abscond) without giving evidence. The warrant is simply for apprehension and committal to prison until the date of the trial, unless he finds caution for his appearance or is released unconditionally.[2] In summary cases the matter is regulated by statute: by s 320 of the 1975 Act, where a witness after being duly cited fails to appear at the diet fixed for his attendance and no just excuse is offered on his behalf, the court may issue a warrant for his apprehension; or the court, if satisfied by evidence on oath that a witness is not likely to attend to give evidence without being compelled to do so, may issue a warrant for his apprehension in the first place. Section 321(5) provides that such a warrant implies warrant to officers of law to search for and apprehend the witness, and to detain him in a police station house, police cell, or other convenient place, until the date fixed for the hearing of the case, unless sufficient security be found to the amount fixed in the warrant for the appearance of such witness at all diets of court.

It has been suggested that a warrant for the apprehension of a witness who fails to attend after being duly cited is one which should be exercised with caution and only after an enquiry has been made as to the reasons for non-attendance.[3] In all cases the citation of the witness will require to be established by the production of the relative execution making it clear that the witness has been properly cited, either by the police or by other officers of law. A witness is (in practice) entitled to forty-eight hours notice of the diet which he is to attend, and accordingly that this amount of notice was given requires to be established.[4] Frequently in summary cases neither side is able to produce the relative execution of citation; this slack practice often hinders the due course of justice.

1   Alison *Practice*, 398.
2   *Hume* II, 375.
3   *Renton and Brown* para 13-90.
4   The 1975 Act fixes no induciae for witnesses, but a period of forty-eight hours is taken as the minimum necessary.

2.09   The case law on this topic is instructive. In *HM Advocate v Bell*[1] a witness who fled from his home rather than give evidence at a High Court trial was arrested on a warrant while the trial was still in progress. He duly gave evidence and was released from custody, only to find himself later as the subject of a petition at the instance of the Crown alleging contempt of court, of which he was later convicted.[2] In *Sergeant, Petitioner*[3] a witness failed to attend a trial which then required to be adjourned. The sheriff granted a warrant for his arrest and fixed caution at £200. On the warrant being executed the witness brought a petition to the *nobile officium* of the High Court of Justiciary seeking his release and stating that he could not find the security ordered due to his low income. The High Court varied the warrant, reducing the caution to £10. In an extreme case, a warrant to arrest may be granted without reference to caution. So, where the sheriff has reasonable grounds for apprehending that there is a real risk of a witness not obeying a citation, a warrant in unconditional terms may be granted. This was done in *Stallworth v HM Advocate*[4] in spite of a defence submission that the witness had been assaulted and subjected to threats from persons which he regarded as an attempt to dissuade him from giving evidence at the trial. The test in *Stallworth* was applied in *Gerrard*, Petitioner[5] where a witness who had failed to travel from Liverpool to Dumfries to attend a trial to which he had been cited and for which journey he had been put in funds, nonetheless failed to appear, there being a history of reluctance to co-operate on his part.

As has been indicated, either party may apply for a warrant, although applications on the part of the defence are uncommon. If procedure by petition requires to be adopted, it must be stressed that it falls into two stages: firstly there must be some information as to the circumstances presented to the sheriff; having considered the petition and examined on oath the officer concerned, the sheriff grants warrant for the apprehension of witness and his production in court for examination.[6] Only at that stage may the witness be further committed in custody to be detained until the trial of the accused, or until he finds caution, if such is allowed. The witness therefore has an opportunity of explaining his position to the sheriff immediately after his arrest. In summary cases in spite of the terms of s 321(5) of the 1975 Act, any witness apprehended under a warrant is brought before the court on the next lawful day and the question of release with or without caution is examined then, as is the question of contempt.

1   1936 JC 89.
2   The position regarding witnesses in summary cases who fail to attend is covered by s 344(1) of the 1975 Act, which provides for a finding of contempt of court. This provision is often invoked after a witness has been apprehended on a warrant.
3   1989 SCCR 448.
4   1978 SLT 93.
5   1984 SLT 108.
6   *Stallworth v HM Advocate* 1978 SLT 93.

Miscellaneous apprehension warrants under statute

2.10   A number of statutory provisions empower courts to grant apprehension warrants in a variety of circumstances. The following sets of provisions are perhaps those most commonly encountered in practice, but others are invoked from time to time.

Means enquiry warrants

Section 398(2) of the 1975 Act provides for the issue of a warrant by a summary court for the purpose of enabling enquiry to be made as to the reason why a fine has not been paid; s 398(3) allows the court to issue such a warrant if the defaulter has failed to answer a citation to appear at a 'means enquiry' court; and s 398(4) provides for the style of such warrant.[1] By virtue of s 194 of the 1975 Act, these provisions also apply in solemn cases.

Breach of probation

Sections 186(1) and 387(1) of the 1975 Act provide that if, on information on oath from the officer supervising an offender who has been made the subject of a probation order, it appears to the court by which the order was made or to the appropriate court that the probationer has failed to comply with any of the requirements of the order, that court may *inter alia* issue a warrant for his arrest.[2] On being brought to the court, he may be dealt with in a variety of ways if the breach of probation is proved.[2] A warrant may also be granted for the apprehension of a probationer who has been convicted by a court in any part of Great Britain of an offence committed during the probation period and who has been dealt with for that offence.[3] On such warrant being executed, the court which issued the warrant (which will be the court which originally imposed probation or which otherwise has jurisdiction over the probationer) may deal with the probationer for the original offence by conviction and/or sentence.[4]

Breach of community service order

Where the local authority officer assigned under the Community Service by Offenders (Scotland) Act 1978 to act as community service officer for an offender on whom an order under the Act is made gives evidence on oath that the offender has failed to comply with the order, the court may issue a warrant for his arrest.[5] On his appearance under the warrant he may be dealt with in respect of any breach of the order which is admitted or proved.[6]

Escaped prisoners and mental patients

Sections 13 and 322 of the 1975 Act provide for the issue by a sheriff or a justice of the peace of a warrant for the apprehension of (i) an offender at large from a prison or other institution to which the Prisons (Scotland) Act 1989 (or equivalent English and Northern Irish legislation) applies in which he is required to be detained after being convicted of an offence or (ii) a convicted mental patient liable to be re-taken under the appropriate sections of the mental health legislation applicable to his case. Although such warrant may be issued by a justice, as well as a sheriff, it is for apprehension and production before the sheriff, who thereafter is empowered to take appropriate action.[7]

1   Section 38A of the Criminal Law Act 1977 covers the question of execution of such warrants in different parts of the United Kingdom.
2   See *Renton and Brown* para 17-64.
3   1975 Act, ss 187(1), 388(1).
4   See *Renton and Brown* para 17-68.
5   Community Service by Offenders (Scotland) Act 1978, s 4(1).
6   Ibid, s 4(2).
7   1975 Act, ss 13(2), 322(2).

WARRANTS FOR CITATION

Introduction

2.11   Another important area of the criminal justice system which can only function through legal means of enforcement is that relating to the requirement of attendance at court. Although some criminal proceedings can proceed in the absence of key participants such as the accused or a witness, that they proceed at all is frequently the consequence of an 'executive' warrant whereby attendance is required not by apprehension but by citation. Three main classes of individual are made the subject of such warrants: accused persons, witnesses and jurors. Citation itself is a complex matter, redolent with technical provisions of law, but it is not the main subject matter of the following paragraphs.[1] These are restricted to an examination of the types of warrant upon which citation is achieved.

1   On citation in criminal cases, see *Renton and Brown* under the relevant index headings.

Accused persons: general provisions

2.12 An accused person may be given formal notice that his attendance is required at a diet in his case by means of a citation proceeding by virtue of an appropriate legal warrant. In solemn proceedings the only warrant to cite the accused which is granted is that which relates to a trial diet. The matter is governed by s 69 of the 1975 Act, which provides for the issue by the sheriff clerk of the district in which a trial on indictment in the sheriff court is to be held, or by the Clerk of Justiciary in respect of High Court trials, of a warrant to officers of law to cite persons accused, along with witnesses and jurors. Such warrant is in the form prescribed by Schedule 1 of the Act of Adjournal (Consolidation) 1988; provision is also made for executions of citation in respect of the accused and others cited. Such a warrant, authenticated by the signature of the clerk, or a duly certified copy thereof, is sufficient warrant to all officers of law competent.[1] It is upon this warrant that service of an indictment is effected.[2]

In summary proceedings, accused persons are frequently cited to attend court, but normally only for an initial appearance on the complaint. Any subsequent appearances follow as a result of other orders made then. By s 315(1) thereof, the 1975 Act itself is sufficient warrant for the citation of the accused (and witnesses) in a summary prosecution to any ordinary sitting of the court or to any special diet fixed by the court or any adjournment thereof. A large number of cases proceed annually in summary criminal courts by the service of a complaint with any accompanying schedules or notices under cover of a formal citation to attend a particular court on a particular day. If this method of proceeding is adopted, no application for a warrant requires to be made in any individual case before service is attempted, but the complaint must be signed before warrant under the Act can be invoked.[3]

1 1975 Act, s 69.
2 Except in cases where an accused pleads guilty by virtue of the accelerated procedure under s 102 of the 1975 Act.
3 *Stewart v Lang* (1894) 1 Adam 493.

Warrants to cite accused for statutory contraventions

2.13 Mention has already been made of the rule that summary proceedings for statutory contraventions must, unless the statute or order under which the proceedings are brought fixes any other period, be commenced within six months after the contravention occurred.[1] If the accused is cited properly within this period, then the warrant to do so which is being relied on is the warrant under s 315(1) of the 1975 Act. If however there is no actual commencement of the proceedings within that period by effective citation, the proceedings may nonetheless be saved by the provisions of s 331(3) which provides for 'deemed' commencement on the date 'on which a warrant to apprehend or to cite the accused is granted, if such warrant is executed without undue delay.' The question of delay is considered later, but it is important to note that s 331(3) refers to the *granting* of a warrant to apprehend or to cite. Since no such warrant is *granted* if the prosecutor relies on s 315(1) in cases of 'actual' commencement of proceedings, what warrant is to be relied on in cases of 'deemed' commencement under s 331? The answer became clear as a result of *Keily v Tudhope*.[2] There, actual postal citation within the six month period was attempted but the complaint was returned marked 'not known at this address'. When the complaint called, a warrant for the arrest of the accused was granted under s 314(1) of the 1975 Act. This warrant was granted before the time bar but not executed for about six weeks, by which time the six month period had been exceeded. No explanation was given for such a delay. The sheriff held that the proceedings were timeous, but on appeal the High Court held *inter alia* that the relevant warrant for the purposes of s 331(3) was the warrant to arrest; that s 315 had no application to s 331(3) and that proceedings could be deemed to be commenced by the grant of a warrant to cite only where a diet was assigned in terms of s 314(1)(a), the deemed date of commencement being the date of the order assigning the diet. It was also held that since no explanation had been offered for the delay in executing the warrant to arrest, the Crown could not invoke s 331(3). Section 314(1)(a) provides for the assignation of a diet to which an accused may be cited, where a complaint is laid before a judge for that purpose; if this is done, the date of that diet is the date of the 'granting' of the warrant to cite for the purposes of the 'deemed commencement' provisions of s 331(3).[3] In *Keily v Tudhope* there was no assigned diet under s 314(1)(a); the operative warrant there was the warrant to arrest granted in terms of s 314(1)(b) when the complaint called, but which was not executed timeously, with the result that there was no 'deemed' commencement of the proceedings.[4]

1   1975 Act, s 331(1).
2   1986 SCCR 251, 1987 SLT 99n.
3   See *Lockhart v Bradley* 1977 SLT 5.
4   1986 SCCR 251 at 255, 256.

Delay in execution of warrant to cite

2.14   As has been noted, 'deemed' commencement of summary proceedings for a statutory contravention only occurs if the warrant to apprehend or cite is executed without undue delay.[1] The question thus arises: what degree of delay will nullify the proceedings? Broadly speaking, the delay in execution must not be for any reason for which the prosecutor is responsible. Fault or slackness on his part will probably be fatal. The case law on this subject is discussed fully in the standard texts and it is proposed only to mention here the leading authorities.[2] These relate to cases where a warrant to cite has been granted, as opposed to a warrant to apprehend, but the principles are the same. In *Smith v Peter Walker & Son (Edinburgh) Ltd.*[3] a warrant to cite the accused was granted shortly before the expiry of the six month period. It was executed almost three weeks later, at a point in time two weeks after the time bar had been reached. It was held that the delay in execution was 'undue' and that the proceedings had not been commenced timeously. The court commented that it was for the prosecutor to justify non-timeous execution; the expression 'undue delay' carried with it the implication that any delay in service might be regarded as excessive if no justification for it could be seen from the circumstances of the case.

In *Beattie v Tudhope*[4] the prosecutor obtained a warrant to cite on the last day of the prescriptive period relative to the offence charged. Service thereafter took six days; a plea to the competency of the proceedings on the basis of undue delay was repelled by the sheriff after hearing evidence as to the circumstances. On appeal, the High Court held that the question was one of fact, circumstances and degree for the sheriff and that in this case it could not be said he had exercised his discretion wrongly. The facts turned on the application of local procedure in Glasgow for the personal service of complaints by police officers in the context of the normal system adopted, all of which was examined in the course of proof.

A similar close examination of the circumstances was carried out in *McNeillie v Walkingshaw*,[5] where a delay of two days in the execution of the relative warrant was held not to be 'undue'. In spite of a failure by the prosecutor to alert the police to the urgency of serving a complaint which was about to become time-barred, the High Court refused to interfere with the exercise of discretion by the sheriff who heard the full facts and decided the issue on the information before him.

From these cases (which are merely illustrative of a line of authority) it is apparent that the statute countenances some delay in execution of a warrant; only if the delay becomes 'undue' are the proceedings tainted. As the onus is on the prosecutor to show that there has not been undue delay, he may require to lead evidence as to the circumstances in which it has arisen.[6]

1 1975 Act, s 331(3).
2 See eg *Renton and Brown* paras 13-08, 13-09.
3 1978 JC 44.
4 1984 SCCR 198.
5 1990 SCCR 428.
6 The matter can however be dealt with on the basis of *ex parte* statements: see *Kennedy v Carmichael* 1991 SCCR 458.

Warrants to cite witnesses for precognition

2.15 It is a matter of moral duty of every person to give a precognition as to the circumstances of his involvement as a witness in the course of criminal case, both to Crown and to the defence alike.[1] If therefore a potential witness fails to answer a request from the procurator fiscal or from the defence legal advisers to give a precognition, his attendance may be enforced by virtue of a warrant.[2]

In the case of witnesses required to give information to the Crown, in solemn cases the initiating petition includes a crave for warrant to cite witnesses for precognition, but in summary cases, no such formality pertains, presumably because in summary cases most witnesses led by the Crown have never been precognosced, as opposed to having given a police statement. But a warrant to cite for precognition can be obtained at any stage, even before the arrest of the accused, although such a warrant would be granted only in cases of serious or unascertained crime.[3] If necessary, a precognition on oath may be required, in which case the witness is cited to attend at a specified diet. It may be that a warrant can be granted for apprehension of a person who fails to attend such a diet, although there are no cases on the point.

Persons failing to give a voluntary precognition to the defence may also be cited to appear for precognition on oath before the sheriff. By s 9(1) of the Criminal Justice (Scotland) Act 1980 it is provided:

'9(1): The sheriff may, on the application of an accused, grant warrant to cite any person (other than a co-accused), who is alleged to be a witness in relation to any offence of which the accused has been charged, to appear before the sheriff in chambers at such time or place as shall be specified in the citation, for precognition on oath by the accused or his solicitor in relation to that offence, if the court is satisfied that it is reasonable to require such precognition on oath in the circumstances.'

It is an offence to fail, without reasonable cause, to attend in response to such a citation, having been given at least forty-eight hours notice of the diet;[4] it is also an offence to attend but to refuse to give information within one's knowledge or to produce evidence in one's possession, or to prevaricate in evidence.[5]

These sections require to be invoked from time to time by defence solicitors faced with reluctant witnesses. However, a divergence of judicial approach is evident from the reported cases. In *Low v McNeill*[6] it was held that the power under s 9 should be exercised with caution and only in unusual and exceptional circumstances analogous to those in which the Crown seeks to precognosce on oath; the circumstances must be such that it is reasonable that a precognition should be given on oath, not merely that it is reasonable that the witness should be required to give a precognition. In the circumstances of that case, the application under s 9 was refused; in his Note the sheriff discussed at length the practical difficulties which he foresaw if s 9 became widely used. In *Cirignaco v Lockhart*[7] an application was also refused on the basis that the applicant had failed to pass the test set out in *Low v McNeill*; in particular it was held that s 9 could not be invoked at an early stage in the criminal process when the accused had not yet been fully committed and where a precognition taken in response to a warrant under s 9 was thought would assist in a subsequent bail application. However, a somewhat different view was taken in *Brady v Lockhart*.[8] There, an application under s 9 was granted; it was held that the purpose of the section was to allow the defence to prepare on equal terms with the Crown and that the words 'on oath' in s 9(1) did not mean that it was restricted to cases where perjury was anticipated. The sheriff disagreed with the views expressed in *Low v McNeill* and *Cirignaco v Lockhart*, stating that the fact that the precognition is to be taken on oath was merely for administrative purposes so that the exercise could be a meaningful one, and of some value to the defence.

In that rather uneasy state the law remains. Petitions under s 9 continue to be uncommon, presumably because in some cases the Crown co-operate with the defence in making available the information they have as to what the witness is expected to say.

An application for an order under s 9 is made by petition in the form set out in Form 1 or 2, whichever is appropriate, of Schedule 1 to the Act of Adjournal (Consolidation) 1988, which Act also regulates procedure.[9] If the warrant is granted, citation must be made by personal service and an execution of service must be produced at the diet.[10]

As well as providing for criminal penalties in the event of failure to appear, s 9(2) of the 1980 Act provides in such a case for the issue of a warrant for the apprehension of the person concerned, ordering him to be brought before a sheriff for a precognition on oath. Paragraph 7(2) of the Act of Adjournal provides that execution of such warrant:

(a) shall be executed by an officer of law, instructed by the accused or his solicitor;

(b) may proceed on a copy of the petition and warrant duly signed by the sheriff clerk.

1 *HM Advocate v Morison* (1893) 1 Adam 114 at 135.
2 *Forbes v Main* (1908) 5 Adam 503. The view has also been expressed that it is competent to cite witnesses to attend an identification parade: see *Wilson v Tudhope* 1985 SCCR 339.
3 *Forbes v Main op cit*, per Lord Justice-Clerk Macdonald. In *K, Petitioner* 1986 SCCR 709 a warrant was granted at the instance of an accused for the medical examination of a child whom he had allegedly assaulted.
4 Criminal Justice (Scotland) Act 1980, s 9(2).
5 Ibid, s 9(4).
6 1981 SCCR 243.
7 1985 SCCR 157.
8 1985 SCCR 349.
9 Act of Adjournal (Consolidation) 1988 paras 5 to 9, 93 to 97.
10 Ibid paras 7(1), 95(1).

Warrants to cite witnesses for trial

2.16 Citation of witnesses is always carried out under warrant. In solemn cases, the matter is governed by s 69 of the 1975 Act, which has already been mentioned in relation to accused persons. The section also provides for forms of execution of citation.[1] In summary cases, s 315 of the 1975 Act provides that the Act itself is sufficient warrant for the citation of witnesses to any ordinary sitting of the court or to any special diet fixed by the court or any adjournment thereof. These sections relate to the citation of witnesses both for the Crown and the defence.

1 See Criminal Procedure (Scotland) Act 1887, Sch D.

Jurors

2.17 In a case prosecuted under solemn procedure, the warrant to cite jurors for the trial, whether in the sheriff court or the High Court of Justiciary, is that which is issued under s 69 of the 1975 Act. As has been noted, this applies also to accused persons and witnesses.[1]

1   See *supra* paras 2.12 and 2.16.

Persons upon whom sentence has been passed

2.18   A warrant to cite someone already sentenced may be necessary in order to bring him back before the court for some purpose. Such warrants are commonly encountered in relation to the situation where the offender has not paid a fine imposed on him, or has apparently breached orders for community service or probation. The relative sections, already discussed under the heading of warrants to apprehend, also provide for warrants for citation.[1]

1   See *supra* para 2.10.

WARRANTS FOR COMMITTAL

Introduction

2.19   Once an accused person has appeared before a competent court, his further disposal depends on his plea, the nature of the case and the form of proceedings. It may be that the matter can be immediately concluded: for example, an accused may be appearing on a summary complaint, plead guilty and be dealt with by way of a fine. In such cases no further warrant is necessary.[1] If however, the case requires to be continued for some reason and the accused requires to appear again, or if the court adopts a custodial disposal, then an appropriate warrant must be granted so that such orders can be enforced. This area of law is frequently ignored by busy practitioners, who rarely take the time to examine the warrants issued; this unfortunate attitude sometimes has the effect of letting errors go undetected.

1   Unless of course the fine is not paid, in which case a means enquiry warrant may be necessary; see *supra* para 2.10.

Pre-trial committal: solemn cases

2.20   Committals in solemn procedure always proceed under warrant, whether for further examination or until liberated in due course of law.[1] The standard form of petition contains the forms of warrant. The first (and sometimes only) committal following the initial appearance of the accused on petition is for further examination. Bail may or may not be allowed at this stage; if bail is not applied for or is refused the committal warrant specifies the institution in which the accused will be incarcerated for the initial period.[2] This period cannot exceed eight days exclusive of the day on which the committal is made and the day when the accused re-appears for the next stage in proceedings, which is committal on a different warrant 'until liberated in due course of law', usually known as full committal.[3] Full committal is unnecessary where bail has previously been allowed.[4]

At full committal, service of the petition and warrants is carried out. This is required by s 22 of the 1975 Act which prohibits full committal without a warrant in writing expressing the particular charge in respect of which the accused is committed. It is also provided that any such warrant for imprisonment which either proceeds on an unsigned information or does not express the particular charge is null and void.[5] A proper warrant of full committal remains in force until the accused is acquitted or sentence is passed. The warrant would however fly off if the accused is liberated by proper legal authority, either on the instructions of the Lord Advocate prior to indictment or plea, or after a plea of guilty but before sentence.[6] Where a diet is deserted *pro loco et tempore*, or is postponed or adjourned, or an order issued for the trial to take place at a different place from that first given notice of, no new warrant is necessary for the incarceration of the accused, but the full committal warrant on which he is at the time in custody continues in force.[7] It has been held that an invalid committal warrant does not vitiate a conviction on an indictment regularly served and a trial regularly conducted.[8]

1   See *Renton and Brown* para 5-70.
2   This is normally the nearest institution with facilities for untried prisoners of the particular age or sex of the person concerned, but once committed to the institution, prisoners are sometimes transferred in accordance with rules made under the Prisons (Scotland) Act 1989.
3   See *Herron v A,B,C, and D* 1977 SLT (Sh Ct) 24 where the court refused to commit persons who had been detained in excess of eight days.
4   1975 Act, s 26(4).
5   Ibid, s 22(2).
6   But see 1975 Act, ss 102(3), 110.
7   1975 Act, s 111.
8   *McVey v HM Advocate* (1911) 6 Adam 503.

Pre-trial committal: summary cases

2.21   No formal warrant of commitment is required in summary cases where an accused pleads not guilty and the diet is adjourned for trial, even where bail is refused and the accused is remanded in custody for trial. By s 430(1) of the 1975 Act the finding of a court of summary jurisdiction, as regards both offences at common law and offences under any statute or order must be entered in the record of proceedings, which is sufficient warrant for all execution thereon and for the clerk of court to issue extracts containing such executive clauses as may be necessary for the implement thereof.[1] Special provision is made for the remand and committal of persons under twenty-one years of age.[2] Any warrant of committal to a local authority or to a remand centre must contain specification of the identity of the authority or centre.[2]

1   Such extracts normally contain warrant for detention where this is appropriate, along with warrant to officers of law to convey the accused to whichever custodial establishment is ordered.
2   1975 Act, s 329.

Committal pending sentence

2.22   In solemn proceedings, the original warrant of full commitment extends beyond the date of conviction until sentence is passed upon a person who has pleaded guilty or who has been convicted by the jury.[1] This rule applies whether the accused is sentenced following adjournment under s 179 of the 1975 Act or after a period of deferment under s 219 thereof.[2]

In summary proceedings, just as there is no warrant necessary for committal for trial, there is no warrant necessary for committal pending sentence, and s 430(1) of the 1975 Act equally applies.

1   The committal is 'until liberated in due course of law', on which see *supra* para 2.20. But see 1975 Act, s 110 for the position where sentence is delayed following a plea of guilty.
2   On the distinctions between adjournment and deferment under these sections, see *McRobbie v HM Advocate* 1990 SCCR 767.

Warrants in respect of custodial sentences

2.23   If an accused person is sentenced under solemn procedure to a period of custody, the entry of the sentence in the record of proceedings, signed by the clerk of court, is full warrant and authority for all execution to follow thereon and for the clerk to issue extracts thereof for carrying the same into execution or otherwise.[1] The extract sentence warrant of detention and return of sentence is in the form set out in Form 36 of Schedule 1 to the 1988 Act of Adjournal.[2]

If any custodial sentence is imposed in a summary case, the 1975 Act itself is sufficient warrant for all execution thereon and for the clerk of court to issue extracts containing such executive clauses as may be necessary for implement thereof; and, when imprisonment forms part of any sentence or other judgment, warrant for the apprehension and interim detention of the accused pending his being committed to prison shall, where necessary be implied.[3] An extract of the finding and sentence, in the form, as nearly as may be, of the appropriate form contained in Part V of Schedule 2 to the Summary Jurisdiction (Scotland) Act 1954 is a sufficient warrant for the apprehension and commitment of the accused, and no such extract shall be void or liable to be set aside on account of any error or defect in part of form.[4]

These provisions apply equally to adult and non-adult offenders.[5]

1   1975 Act, s 217(2).
2   1988 Act of Adjournal, rule 83(2).
3   1975 Act, s 430(1).
4   Ibid, s 440.
5   Young offenders are not sentenced to imprisonment, but the form of any custodial sentence imposed on a young offender has no bearing on the nature of the extract warrant which is issued, only its form.

Warrants in cases of persons suffering from mental disorder

2.24   The 1975 Act contains a number of provisions whereby a person suffering (or thought to be suffering) from mental disorder may be committed to hospital, either for pre-trial enquiry into his condition, or as a disposal following the establishment of his condition or the determination of his guilt or innocence.[1] The whole subject of mental disorder in relation to criminal procedure is dealt with fully elsewhere;[2] suffice it to say here that a warrant is always necessary wherever compulsory admission to hospital is the order of the court, for whatever purposes or period.

1   See eg 1975 Act, ss 25(1), 330(1), (pre-trial); ss 175(1), 376(1), (post-trial).
2   *Renton and Brown*, ch 20.

3. Search warrants at common law

SEARCH OF THE PERSON

Introduction

3.01 Warrants for the personal search of an individual are commonly granted in practice. Such a warrant often accompanies a warrant to apprehend, especially where criminal proceedings are being commenced by virtue of the latter, but occasionally a warrant for personal search may be applied for once the criminal process is more advanced. As a matter of general law the police have no right to search anyone prior to arrest, although they acquire that right after that point, whether or not a warrant has been granted. But many statutes provide exceptions to this generality.[1] In particular, the police have the same powers of search in relation to a person detained under s 2 of the Criminal Justice (Scotland) Act 1980 as they do in relation to arrested persons.[2] The law on the limited rights of the police to carry out a personal search of an individual without a warrant is of course outwith the scope of this book, and the problems inherent in those rules of law do not arise when a warrant to search is granted by a court.[3] In such a situation, as in all cases where a warrant is granted, the acts authorised by the warrant acquire their legality by virtue of the fact that they proceed under the authority of an independent legal officer. Only if the warrant is suspended are the actings done thereunder open to challenge; but in all cases evidence illegally obtained may still be admitted in a subsequent trial.[4]

1 On statutory warrants to search, see *infra* Pt 4.
2 Criminal Justice (Scotland) Act 1980, s 2(5)(b).
3 On search without warrant, see *Renton and Brown* paras 5-30, 5-36.
4 See generally *infra* Pt 5.

What is a 'personal search'?

3.02 The term 'personal search' used in the context of a police enquiry is something of a misnomer. A search of the person extends beyond the mere examination of the external surfaces of the body, the clothes worn by the individual concerned and his personal effects. In a wider sense, a search encompasses such activities as taking finger-prints[1] and rubbings from the hands;[2] examination of the mouth and teeth;[3] examination of the hair, including the pubic hair;[4] the removal of material from under the fingernails;[5] and the scrutiny of material found at the external parts of the body orifices. Indeed, 'looking for evidence' which may be gleaned from the body may reach even further to an internal examination conducted either by the operation of external technology such as an X-ray or other scan, or by medical operation by the insertion of implements designed to elicit informa-tion. The latter cannot really be described as a 'personal search', but such exceptional procedures are sometimes encountered.[6] No doubt they would have seemed incomprehensible to Hume and Alison, but in fact their legal validity today flows from the same general principles which those institutional writers identified and from which the law has developed. A warrant may be granted for a personal search or examination across this entire spectrum; indeed the categories of such investigatory techniques are probably never closed.

1   *Adair v McGarry* 1933 JC 72.
2   *Bell v Hogg* 1967 JC 49.
3   *Hay v HM Advocate* 1968 JC 40.
4   *McGlennan v Kelly* 1989 SCCR 352, 1989 SLT 832.
5   *McGovern v HM Advocate* 1950 JC 33.
6   See *infra* para 3.05.

What force can be used to carry out a personal search?

3.03   It is in relation to personal search that the issue of force discussed earlier arises most sharply. It has already been suggested that in the absence of any specific statutory provisions authorising the use of force in the execution of a statutory warrant, Scots law recognises the use of 'reasonable' force in the carrying out of a personal search.[1] This, it is submitted, must be the common law position also, for the reasons advanced already. But, as will be apparent from the following discussion of the various types of searches and examinations which may be conducted under warrant, what is 'reasonable' probably has to be judged in the light of the procedure proposed and against the background of the competing interests involved. It is impossible to be more than tentative in this area, given the lack of authority in both criminal and civil law.

1   See *supra* paras 1.22–1.24.

Warrants to search or examine a suspect

3.04   As is often emphasised the police have no common law power to search someone suspected of crime, although if such an illegal search is carried out, the fruits thereof may nonetheless be admitted in evidence at a later trial.[1] It is a corollary of the general rule that a warrant will not normally be granted to search someone who is yet to be arrested and charged, however strong the police suspicion may be. But in exceptional cases only, such a warrant is competent, provided the circumstances are truly special. There appear to be no reported cases on this point until 1968; until then the general proposition that to search a suspect was illegal was well established. In *Jackson v Stevenson*[2] the Lord Justice-General observed that he knew of no authority for ascribing to constables the right to make tentative searches, and that they seemed contrary to constitutional principle. He continued:

'If the constable requires to make such a search, it can only be because without it he is not justified in apprehending; and, without a warrant, to search a person not liable to apprehension seems palpably illegal.'[3]

These *dicta* underpin the decisions in *Adamson v Martin*[4] and *McGovern v HM Advocate*[5] and encapsulate the general law.

1   On the question of admissibility, see *infra* Pt 5.
2   (1897) 2 Adam 255; 24 R(J) 38.
3   24 R(J) 38 at 41.
4   1916 SC 319.
5   1950 JC 33.

3.05   But in *Hay v HM Advocate*[1] a sheriff granted a warrant to convey a murder suspect to a dental hospital and to allow two dental surgeons to make a further dental examination of him, his teeth impressions having already been taken. The purpose behind the application was to discover whether bite marks on the victim's breast could assist in the identification of the person responsible for the crime. As a result of the dental examination, Hay was charged with the murder. At his trial, the legality of the warrant and the evidence obtained thereunder came under close scrutiny, but objections thereto were repelled and the accused convicted. On appeal, the High Court held that the warrant had been properly obtained and the evidence properly admitted. But the Lord Justice-General made it clear that a warrant of the limited kind used in that case would only be granted in special circumstances.

It is very unlikely that a warrant to search or examine externally the person of a suspect will very often be encountered in practice. *Hay v HM Advocate* predates the passing of the Criminal Justice (Scotland) 1980 Act; under s 2(5) thereof, not only may a constable exercise in respect of a detainee the same powers of search as are available following an arrest; he is also empowered to take fingerprints, palmprints and such other prints and impressions as he may, having regard to the circumstances of the suspected offence, reasonably consider appropriate. Accordingly, the police are far better advised nowadays to exercise their powers of detention under the Act rather than ask the procurator fiscal to obtain the necessary warrant, unless the circumstances are wholly exceptional and it is sought to carry out some highly unusual test which cannot be completed within the six hour detention period.[2]

One such exceptional situation occurs from time to time in drugs cases, although there is no reason in principle why it should not occur in other cases also. This is where an internal examination of a suspect is required to ascertain whether potentially incriminating material may be concealed within his person. Where drugs are suspected of having been secreted within the body either by ingestion or insertion, warrant for medical examination is sometimes necessary. In such cases an application is presented by the procurator fiscal for a warrant to officers of law to convey the suspect (who will have been detained under s 23(2) of the Misuse of Drugs Act 1971) to hospital for examination for the presence of controlled drugs within his person. A style of such application is to be found in the Appendix to this book;[3] there are as yet no reported cases in which the validity of such a warrant has been challenged. It must be stressed that any such warrant is granted at common law, even although the crime suspected may be a contravention of statute and the status of the suspect as a detainee flows also from statutory provision. Such warrants are to be distinguished from those which may be granted under the specific provisions of the Criminal Justice (Scotland) Act 1987 to officers of HM Customs and Excise in relation to drug smuggling offences.

1   1968 JC 40.
2   But see *Morris v MacNeill* 1991 SCCR 722.
3   See *infra* p128.

Warrants to search an arrested person

3.06   All that need be noted here is that the normal form of warrant to arrest, whether proceeding on a petition case or summary complaint, is invariably accompanied by warrant to search the person. In petition cases, this is a matter of common law.[1] In summary cases, the matter is regulated by s 314(1) of the 1975 Act; the procurator fiscal often requests what is known as an 'initiating warrant', the normal form of which includes both warrant to arrest and to search.[2]

1   See *Renton and Brown* para 5-30.
2   On apprehension warrants, see *supra* para 2.01ff.

Warrants for search or examination after commencement of proceedings

3.07   Once an accused person has appeared in court, whether on petition or summary complaint, he acquires certain rights as the judicial process continues. The integrity of his person is generally protected against further examination, on the basis that having been charged with a crime he cannot be put in the situation of being required to assist the Crown case any further. Indeed it was held in *Smith v Innes*[1] (a summary case) that a warrant cannot be granted to take the fingerprints of someone who has appeared on complaint and pleaded not guilty. However, warrants are sometimes granted in practice for the purposes of taking a blood sample from an accused person who is being prosecuted under solemn procedure and has been committed for further examination either in custody or on bail. In the latter case, such a warrant seeks also apprehension for the limited purpose of taking the accused to a suitable place for the sample to be taken. There are no reported examples of cases where such warrants have been challenged.

There have also been a number of cases where warrants have been granted after the full committal of an accused person under solemn procedure. The first of these was *HM Advocate v Milford*[2] where Sheriff Macphail granted a warrant to take a blood sample from an accused person who had been fully committed on a charge of rape. In *Wilson v Milne*,[3] the High Court refused a Bill of Suspension in respect of a similar warrant granted after full committal, holding that the granting of the warrant would not disturb the delicate balance which must be maintained between the public interest and the interests of the accused. In both of these cases, exceptional circumstances were said to exist, justifying departure from the general rule that an accused person, once committed for trial, cannot be forced to give or provide evidence against himself. The whole matter was considered fully in *Lees v Weston*[4] where a warrant was sought to take fingerprints from an accused who had been fully committed, there having been an administrative error on the part of the police which had resulted in a failure to take them at the time of arrest. The sheriff refused the warrant upon the view that the Crown were trying to improve their case by trying to get round a police blunder, and that the court should be slow to cure the errors of public servants in the investigation of crime. This decision was reversed on appeal; the High Court reiterated that such a warrant would only be granted in special circumstances; that the whole circumstances must be considered and the public interest in the investigation and suppression of crime must be weighed against the interests of the accused; that in this case the error by the police had been excusable; and that insufficient weight had been given to the relatively minor nature of the invasion of the accused's bodily integrity involved in taking fingerprints as against the seriousness of the charges against him. The Lord Justice-Clerk observed that to require an accused person to provide finger impressions was materially different from interrogating an accused person and requiring him to answer questions; no positive action was required of a person whose fingerprints were being taken. The matter is one for the discretion of the sheriff hearing the application; if it can be shown that he misused his discretion, then the High Court will intervene. In *McGlennan v Kelly*[5] a warrant to take a sample of the pubic hair of an accused charged with rape was refused by the sheriff. An earlier sample had been taken at the time of arrest (almost two years previously) but comparison with hairs found at the *locus* had proved neutral. The Crown appeal against this decision was refused; in light of the delay between the provision of the original sample and the seeking of the warrant, the Crown failed to show that the sheriff had so misdirected himself as to vitiate his decision. But in *Currie v McGlennan*[6] a warrant to have four accused who had been fully committed on a charge of murder conveyed from prison to a police office to stand on an identification parade was granted by the sheriff; his decision was upheld on appeal. The basis for this was that special circumstances had been shown: although an earlier parade had been held before full committal, two new witnesses had been located after that date and the circumstances of the alleged murder were particularly 'chilling, extraordinary and bizarre'.

In *Frame v Houston*[7] the accused sought to suspend a warrant ordaining him to provide a sample of hair for comparison with those found on a mask used during the course of a robbery. An earlier sample had been taken but this was alleged to have been insufficient for comparison. The accused argued that since he had been served with an indictment it was incompetent to require him to provide evidence to assist the case against him. The High Court refused to suspend the warrant, holding that the service of the indictment did not necessarily mean that the case would proceed on that basis; the cut-off point was only reached when the case actually came to trial. Since the granting of the warrant was within the discretion of the sheriff and since he had taken all material factors into account, the appeal failed.

This tract of authority clearly indicates that each case must be dealt with on its own merits; in particular the fact of full committal seems to have little relevance to such decisions, even although it might be thought that by seeking full committal the Crown would be saying to the court, in effect, that there was sufficient evidence to warrant putting the accused on trial. While it might be argued that the public interest should not require obstacles to be placed in the way of the Crown in seeking to make a *prima facie* case stronger, the private interest of the accused cannot be discounted entirely. In this regard, there is undoubtedly force in the argument that while passive steps by the accused, such as the giving of fingerprints, blood or hair do not involve gross invasion of bodily integrity, there may be difficult cases where more than just passive co-operation may be necessary to serve the purpose of the examination. Indeed, it is open to question whether giving fingerprints under a warrant is in fact a passive act; it may, after all, involve the use of some force and could be resisted by a determined accused. And if an accused cannot be compelled to stand up in the dock to assist the Crown in identifying him in the course of a trial, some might ask why should he be compelled to give a fingerprint or other sample after charge or committal but before the trial?[8]

1   1984 SCCR 119.
2   1973 SLT 12.
3   1975 SLT (Notes) 26.
4   1989 SCCR 177; 1989 SLT 446.
5   1989 SCCR 352, 1989 SLT 832.
6   1989 SCCR 466.
7   1991 SCCR 436.
8   See *Beattie v Scott* 1990 SCCR 296.

Execution of personal search under warrant

3.08   Since a warrant to search an individual is a usual accompaniment of a warrant to apprehend, the search under warrant is executed after the apprehension has taken place. There are no statutory guidelines as to how a personal search is to be carried out, but it is often carried out on the spot[1] or sometimes later at the police office. Good police practice requires that the search be carried out by one officer in the presence of another, so that there may be corroboration of what is actually found. Standard police procedure also forbids the searching of a female prisoner by a male officer; as will be seen, this is also a legal prohibition in relation to some statutory warrants.[2]

1   *Jackson v Stevenson* (1897) 2 Adam 255.
2   See *infra* paras 4.36, 4.47.

SEARCH OF PREMISES

Introduction

3.09   As with personal search, the police have no general power to enter private premises without a warrant to search for stolen property or other articles which might establish the commission of a crime or implicate a particular person. There however the comparison with personal search ends, for while a warrant will not normally be granted to search a person suspected of crime, warrants are frequently granted at common law for the search of premises prior to the arrest of anyone, provided the usual rules as to validity are complied with: in particular, the warrant must specify the articles to which the search is directed and the places to be searched, a warrant in general terms being illegal.[1] There are in addition a large number of statutory provisions under which warrants to search may be granted,[2] but, as will be seen later, common law principles underpin that whole area of statute law.

1   On the general requirements of a valid warrant, see supra para 1.10ff.
2   See *infra* Pt 4.

Arrest and charge unnecessary

3.10   It was conclusively established in *Stewart v Roach*[1] that it is not illegal to grant or to execute a warrant to search for stolen goods in the premises of a person who has not been apprehended nor charged with an offence. In that case, a Court of Seven Judges was convened in order to establish this point which arose in an action for damages against a police officer involved in the search of the houses owned by the two pursuers. At the time of the searches, each pursuer was merely the subject of an anonymous letter to the police in which each was named as having been responsible for pilfering from their place of work, but neither had been arrested or charged. Holding that the latter steps were unnecessary as prerequisites of the granting of a search warrant, the court observed that it was difficult to see on principle why the lesser invasion of the pursuers' rights involved in a search of their houses for stolen goods should be objectionable simply because the more extreme step of charging or apprehending them had not been taken; the court went on to disapprove observations to this effect in an earlier case.[2]

1   1950 SC 318.
2   Ibid at 324 ff.

3.11 Accordingly, if police suspicions are aroused as a result of information received, perhaps from an informer or other sources, that articles forming part of the evidence of a crime are to be found in particular premises, then for obvious reasons they may well decide to apply for a warrant to search in preference to simply requesting the permission of the occupier to do so. The occupier may in any event be a suspect or may become one if incriminating articles are found in his premises. If however the premises to be searched are those in which a person is to be arrested, then the warrant under which the search is to be carried out is craved at the same time as the apprehension warrant[1] and is executed contemporaneously with it.

1   See eg 1975 Act, s 314(1).

What are 'premises'?

3.12 If the search warrant relates to particular premises such as 'the house occupied by Smith at 123 Main Street, Anytown', then the extent of those premises and the boundaries thereof may require to be revealed, if not in the application itself but in submission to the justice of the peace, magistrate or sheriff so that an appropriate warrant can be granted. Obviously no particular problem will arise in relation to an ordinary council house, flat, detached or terraced house. But difficulties may arise in other cases, such as in relation to flats divided into separately occupied bed-sitting rooms. In *McAvoy v Jessop*[1] a warrant was granted to search the 'houses occupied by Thomas McAvoy' following upon an application narrating that stolen property was to be found in two separate houses said to be occupied by him at 31 Melville Street and 7 Hamiltonhill Road, both in Glasgow. When the police went to 31 Melville Street they found it was a flat with a number of nameplates at the door containing various names including that of Thomas McAvoy and of his sister Anne McAvoy who was the person ultimately charged with reset.

The police found the room of Thomas McAvoy, which was empty. His sister arrived thereafter; the police requested access to her room but she explained Thomas McAvoy did not live in it. Nonetheless the police showed her the warrant, entered the room (without objection) and found a stolen video recorder. At the subsequent trial of Anne McAvoy objection was taken to the admissibility of this evidence on the basis that the search was unlawful. This objection was overruled by the trial court but the subsequent conviction for reset was quashed on the basis that warrant authorised only the search of the bedsitting room found to have been occupied by Thomas McAvoy. The trial judge was not entitled to hold (as he had) that the police were in effect carrying out a search of separate rooms in a flat which could be regarded as the family home of Thomas McAvoy. Nor was the irregularity excusable: in the circumstances the police could not properly have taken the view that the warrant authorised them to search the room occupied by Anne McAvoy.

If therefore the police can pinpoint the location of a room in a rooming house where the articles are to be sought, and can state this at the time of the application for the warrant, then clearly the warrant should be restricted to that location. But frequently such accuracy will be difficult to achieve. Likewise, in cases of extensive premises such as a farm with relative outbuildings, or commercial premises, offices or the like, every effort should be made to identify in the warrant as clearly as possible exactly where the search may be carried on.

1   1988 SCCR 172.

Forms of common law warrant to search premises

3.13   Prior to the initiation of criminal proceedings an application for a search warrant is in the form of an 'incidental application' under s 310 of the 1975 Act and usually proceeds upon averments that a crime took place on a particular date and that articles relevant to the police investigation (eg the proceeds of a housebreaking) are to be found at a particular location in premises or a house occupied by a named individual. The usual form of crave is for warrant to a named officer or other officers of law to enter the premises by force if necessary, to secure whichever articles are believed to be related to the crime, and to open shut and lockfast places for this purpose.[1] A full style of application is to be found in the Appendix hereto.[2]

If proceedings are initiated by petition warrant, this includes warrant to search 'the person, repositories and domicile of (the accused) and the house or premises in which he (or they) may be found, and to secure, for the purpose of precognition and evidence, all writs, evidents and articles found therein tending to establish guilt or participation in the crimes foresaid, and for that purpose to make patent all shut and lockfast places.'

If proceedings are initiated by summary complaint, a summary search warrant is in slightly different terms: it authorises search of the person and the 'dwellinghouse and repositories of the accused and any place where he may be found for any documents, articles or property likely to afford evidence of his guilt, or guilty participation in, any offence charged in the complaint, and to take possession of such documents, articles or property.'[3]

1   1975 Act, ss 310, 321(1).
2   See *infra* p125.
3   1975 Act, s 314(1).

Execution of warrant

3.14   If a warrant to search premises is issued, the householder or other occupant should be told of the nature of the warrant before the search commences and be asked to give entry. Unless this precaution is observed, then it does not seem that the officer would be justified in breaking open doors to carry out the search.[1] The officer to whom the warrant was issued should, as a matter of good practice, be in possession of it at the time he executes it and he is bound to show it to the householder or other occupant of the premises, if asked to do so.[2] He is not obliged to part with it to anyone for perusal or inspection, but the duty to exhibit the warrant on demand seems absolute unless, as Alison puts it in the context of an apprehension warrant the demand is made 'in such circumstances as appear to endanger the document, or appearing to have arisen from a desire to snatch it out of his hand or get it destroyed.'[3]

But it does not appear that failure by the officer carrying out the search to have the warrant in his possession at the time will invalidate any search carried out, *provided* that he knows what is in the warrant. This whole matter came before the High Court in *Leckie v Miln*,[4] where officers carrying out a search on the instructions of a senior officer were completely unaware of the contents of the petition warrant upon which an accused had been apprehended. Nonetheless they searched his house and found certain articles which were later produced as evidence at his trial. On appeal, the search was held to have been illegal, on the basis that the police were ignorant of the terms of the warrant; furthermore, the defect was not cured by the consent of the occupier of the accused's house.

The time of day at which a search warrant is executed is always left to the discretion of the police and is never specified in the warrant itself. Alison makes a pertinent comment on this issue :

'And in the execution of this delicate duty, it seems to be a salutary precaution which is recommended in the English law viz, that the search warrant, especially where doors are to be broken open, should be executed as much as possible *in the daytime*, the night being a season of alarm and trepidation, when murder and resistance are likely to ensue from the attempt to enforce such warrants. However this is only a measure of precaution, and it cannot be affirmed that it is illegal or irregular to execute such a warrant at night, which very often is the only season when it is likely to meet with success; but only that in general it is advisable, where it can be done without detriment to justice, to select the day session.'[5]

Operational considerations will therefore determine the time of day at which the police execute a search warrant, and it will therefore be very difficult for a person aggrieved by a search at some inconvenient hour to do very much about it, assuming it can be demonstrated that the police acted in good faith.

1   *Hume* II, 80.
2   Ibid; Alison *Practice*, 117.
3   Alison *Practice*, 124.
4   1981 SCCR 261; 1982 SLT 177.
5   Alison *Practice*, 117.

3.15   By contrast with the absence of many written rules in Scottish procedure, present-day English law provides a battery of safeguards as to the execution of search warrants. Among those contained in the Police and Criminal Evidence Act 1984 ('PACE') is a specific provision that entry and search under a warrant must be at a reasonable hour unless it appears to the constable executing it that the purpose of a search may be frustrated on an entry at a reasonable hour.[1] The sanction for non compliance with this and the other listed safeguards is also spelled out in statute: the entry on or search of the premises is unlawful.[2] Very detailed provisions are made in PACE as to the practice to be followed in an application for a search warrant, as to the necessity of showing that the material to be searched for is reasonably believed to be of substantial value to the investigation of the offence and that *inter alia* it does not consist of or include items subject to legal privilege, 'excluded material' or 'special procedure' material.[3] Extensive definitions are provided of the latter two terms: the former includes various kinds of personal confidential business records and journalistic material, while the latter includes *inter alia* material acquired or created in the course of trade, business or profession and possessed subject to an undertaking to hold it in confidence.[4] As well as all this, PACE provides how a search warrant is to be executed: by whom, when and by what procedure.[5] Even more detail is provided in the relative Code of Practice made under PACE; among the more important provisions in Code B is that which imposes an obligation on a police officer applying for a warrant to take reasonable steps to check that the information upon which he proposes to proceed is accurate, recent and has not been provided maliciously or irresponsibly; an application may not be made on the basis of information from an anonymous source where corroboration has not been sought.[6] Code B also provides detailed guidance as to the conduct of a search itself; among other things a search must be conducted with due consideration for the property and privacy of the occupier of the premises searched, and with no more disturbance than is necessary.[7] Detailed records must be kept; names of all participants must be included.[8]

1   Police and Criminal Evidence Act 1984, s 16(4).
2   Ibid, s 15(1).
3   Ibid, ss 8-14 .
4   Ibid, ss 12, 14.
5   Ibid, s 16.
6   Code B, para 2.
7   Ibid para 5.
8   Ibid para 7.

3.16   The contrast between the formalism of the PACE provisions and the discretionary, wider approach of Scots law could not be more stark. While police officers in Scotland carrying out a search under warrant ought to follow whatever is considered appropriate procedure in their own police areas, whether that procedure is prescribed as a result of national agreement on guidelines or local force directions, in England it is both a matter of primary legislation and of 'following the Code', with the sanction that if the procedure is not carried out, then the fruits of the search may not be admitted in evidence. In the latter area, there is some equivalent to the Scottish position but the general experience of PACE since its enactment shows that it is fertile ground for challenges in court to the actions of the police. It is no exaggeration to say that an avalanche of case law has been spawned by PACE,[1] while in Scotland the absence of detailed provisions allows matters to be looked at more broadly. While the Scots law of warrants is hardly redolent with case law, it is somewhat surprising that the subject of execution of a search warrant has not been productive of more examination; as will be seen later, the emphasis in the case law has been on the evidential question of the admissibility of articles found, rather than the police procedures actually followed.[2]

1 On PACE generally see eg Zander, *The Police and Criminal Evidence Act 1984* (2nd edn 1990, with Supplement 1991).
2 See generally *infra* para 5.01ff.

3.17 A final point which must be made on the question of execution of a search warrant is the extent of the information to be given to the occupier of the premises. Apart from the right to see the warrant, Scots law does not specifically endow the occupier with many other rights to know why the police are executing their warrant. As explained earlier, it is unlikely that he will have been given intimation of the application for the warrant and an opportunity to contest its issue.[1] The occupier would be entitled to ask to see the police warrant cards to satisfy himself that the search warrant was in the possession of those entitled to execute it, but beyond that, he appears to have no other entitlement in the matter, although he can of course ask the police whatever questions he likes; but the police do not appear to be required by law to respond. Again, the absence of any rule is in marked contrast to the PACE provisions which apply in England and Wales. Code B requires a police officer carrying out any search to which the code applies to provide the occupier with a copy of a notice in standard format setting out a variety of information, which notice must be provided in every case unless it is impracticable to do so.[2] The information in the notice, as well as specifying whether the search is made under warrant, or with consent or in exercise of other powers, must also:
(i) summarise the extent of the powers of search and seizure conferred in PACE;
(ii) explain the rights of the occupier and of the owner of the property;
(iii) explain that compensation may be payable in appropriate cases for damage caused in entering and searching premises, and giving the address to which an application for compensation should be directed; and
(iv) stating that a copy of Code B is available to be consulted at any police station.[2]
There are also detailed rules as to when the notice is to be handed over and what must be done if the occupier is not present.[2] In Scotland, there would be nothing to stop the police giving an occupier similar written information as to his rights; indeed it is doubtful whether legislation to require this would even be necessary

if the giving of more than basic information was an agreed police practice. The absence of rules in Scotland sits uneasily alongside Article 8 of the European Convention on Human Rights: if everyone has the right to respect for his private and family life, his home and his correspondence subject only to interference *inter alia* for the prevention of disorder or crime, then perhaps the onus should be on those entitled by law to interfere with the general right to privacy to tell the person involved something more about why his rights are being interfered with and what he is entitled to do by way of response.

1   See *supra* para 1.05.
2   Police and Criminal Evidence Act 1984, Code B, paras 5 to 7, 5 to 8.

4. Statutory warrants and orders for search of persons and property and for recovery of evidence

INTRODUCTION

4.01 The common law forms only part of a wider legal framework under which persons may be searched and property of all kinds and descriptions may be recovered under authority of a warrant or other order. A large number of statutes now provide for the granting of particular warrants, so that the enforcement provisions of these statutes can receive practical effect. But at the outset, one general point must be made: the common law relating to search warrants continues to apply even where the statute renders certain conduct criminal, but provides no machinery for the enforcement of the prohibition. In *MacNeill*[1], the procurator fiscal sought a warrant from the sheriff to search the premises of a limited company in order to seize and examine articles with a view to determining whether to take proceedings against the company under s 51(2) of the Civic Government (Scotland) Act 1982, which makes it an offence to deal in obscene material. The sheriff refused to grant the warrant on the basis that the 1982 Act made no provision for search warrants, but his decision was reversed on appeal. The High Court held that the fiscal's common law right to apply for a search warrant before anyone was charged with an offence applied to statutory offences except when it was excluded or restricted expressly or by necessary implication. Accordingly, the absence of statutory machinery is generally no obstacle to the seeking of a warrant at common law, but the statute requires to be examined to ensure that the common law can be used without restriction.

1   1983 SCCR 450

4.02 What follows is an examination of some of the statutes which expressly provide for the granting of warrants. The vast majority of these give jurisdiction to the sheriff or to a justice of the peace, sometimes only on information being presented on oath. The material herein is not intended to be exhaustive, but includes many of the commonest statutes encountered in regular practice. These are arranged in alphabetical order, commencing with the Bankers' Books Evidence Act 1879, which authorises the issue of certain orders akin to warrants of the more conventional type. In respect of each statute certain background information is given, with a brief comment on ancillary matters and a reference to any case law. Other statutes, less commonly encountered, are simply listed, with reference to the main provisions.[1] Finally, there is a discussion of two exceptional statutes which provide for the granting of a warrant by the Secretary of State.[2]

1   *Infra*, para 4.56 ff.
2   *Infra*, para 4.57 ff.

PARTICULAR STATUTES DISCUSSED

(i) Bankers' Books Evidence Act 1879

Principal object of order: inspection and copying of entries in bankers' books

Background

4.03   In broad general terms a bank has an obligation to keep secret the details of accounts kept for its customers and not to reveal information about the banking transactions which they make. One of the exceptions to this rule is where an order is made by a court for the inspection and copying of the bank's records for the purposes of 'legal proceedings', which term is defined by s10 of the 1879 Act (as amended) as meaning 'any civil or criminal proceeding or inquiry in which evidence is or may be given'. In *Carmichael v Sexton*[1] it was held that the words 'in which evidence is or may be given' only qualified the word 'inquiry' preceding them and not the words 'civil or criminal proceeding'. Accordingly it was competent to make an order under s7 at the petition stage of solemn proceedings, before an indictment was served. There must however be in existence 'proceedings' in court, which requires that a petition or summary complaint must have been presented to the court and at least one order pronounced thereon. So, for example, even if warrant to apprehend the accused has been granted on a petition or complaint and no such apprehension has been carried out or other order made, it would be competent to proceed under s 7.

Section 10 of the 1879 Act defines 'the court' as 'the court, judge, arbitrator, persons or person before whom a legal proceeding is held or taken', while the term 'judge' is restricted to a Lord Ordinary. In the result any holder of judicial office in Scotland before whom proceedings are taken may grant an order under s 7.

The term 'banker's books' has an extended meaning as a result of amendments to s 9(2) of the 1879 Act. It includes ledgers, daybooks, cash-books, account books and other records used in the ordinary business of the bank, whether those records are in written form or are kept on microfilm, magnetic tape, or any other form of mechanical or electronic retrieval mechanism. In one unreported case (*Allan*, Petitioner, Edinburgh Sheriff Court, 3 November 1983) an order was made for recovery of a video film showing a transaction involving the account of an accused facing charges under the Misuse of Drugs Act 1971.[2]

Section 9(1) of the 1879 Act, as amended, defines a 'bank' as
(a) an institution authorised under the Banking Act 1987 or a municipal bank within the meaning of that Act;
(b) a building society (within the meaning of the Building Societies Act 1986);
(c) the National Savings Bank; and
(d) the Post Office, in the exercise of its powers to provide banking services.

The Banking Act 1987 sets out various criteria for the authorisation of the relative institutions, which authorisation can only be given by the Bank of England. The latter is required to produce an annual list of institutions which are authorised; in any event, recognised banks under the Banking Act 1979 are deemed to have been granted authorisation under the 1987 Act. Thus, the question as to whether a particular institution is a bank to which the 1879 Act applies should be capable of easy resolution. Further, s 101 of the 1987 Act provides that in any proceedings a certificate purporting to be signed on behalf of the Bank of England and certifying that a particular person is or is not an authorised institution shall be admissible in evidence, and in Scotland shall be sufficient evidence of the facts stated in the certificate. In *Jessop v Rae*[3] it was held unnecessary for the Crown to produce, at the state of application for an order under s 7, a certificate from the Bank of England that the Royal Bank of Scotland plc was an institution duly authorised. But the High Court left open the question of certification in relation to other institutions. The court observed:

'We are unable to say that no sheriff would ever be entitled to insist on the production of such a certificate before granting an application for an order under s 7. The jurisdiction under this section should always be exercised with care, and it may be that in a particular case the question whether or not an institution is a bank for the purposes of the 1879 Act may be so open to doubt that only a certificate under s 101 (of the 1987 Act) can resolve it. But when he is considering whether or not to insist on the production of a certificate the sheriff must have regard to the nature of the proceedings with which he is concerned, the context of the legislation under which the application is made and the state of common knowledge, if any, about the institution to whose books the application relates.'[4]

The court went on to observe that it was a matter of common (but not judicial) knowledge that all the clearing banks in the United Kingdom at least are 'banks' for the purposes of the 1879 Act, and can be assumed to have the necessary authorisation. Whether other institutions fall within the definition may require to be examined when an application under s 7 is presented.

1   1985 SCCR 33
2   *Allan*, Petitioner, Edinburgh Sheriff Court, 3 November 1983
3   1990 SCCR 228
4   Ibid at p233

Text of s 7 of the Bankers' Books Evidence Act 1879

4.04   Section 7 of the 1879 Act provides:
'On the application of any party to a legal proceeding a court or judge may order that such party be at liberty to inspect and take copies of any entries in a banker's book for any of the purposes of such proceedings. An order under this section may be made either with or without summoning the bank or any other party, and shall be served on the bank three clear days before the same is to be obeyed, unless the court or judge otherwise directs.'

Comment

4.05   Since s 7 of the 1879 Act can be only invoked where proceedings are extant, the question arises whether any intimation of the application is necessary. It is clear as a matter of law that an order may be made without summoning the bank or any other party, but it is at least arguable that intimation ought to be made at least to the accused. In common practice applications are disposed of on the *ex parte* statement of the applicant, but this is open to the criticism that basic fairness requires both sides to be heard. The court may also be assisted by hearing the contradictor to the arguments of the applicant. In *Jessop v Rae*[1] the High Court stated that the question of intimation was discretionary; there might be cases of unusual difficulty in which the bank or some other party should be heard before the application is disposed of.

Style of Application: see Appendix p 133

1   1990 SCCR 228

(ii) Criminal Justice (Scotland) Act 1987: drug smuggling offences

Principal object of warrant: detention for up to seven days

Background

4.06 Quite separate from the powers of the police to act under various drugs warrants by virtue of other statutory provisions are those powers enjoyed by officers of HM Customs and Excise under s 50 of the Criminal Justice (Scotland) Act 1987. The latter powers are invoked only in relation to drug smuggling offences and are confined within strict statutory limitations. Section 50 provides for the detention and search of a person who may be seeking to bring drugs into this country, having ingested or otherwise concealed packages thereof within his body. Under s 50(1) an initial period of detention of twenty-four hours at a customs office or other premises is authorised in a situation where an officer has reasonable grounds for suspecting:

(a)   that a person has committed or is committing a relevant offence; and

(b)   that in connection with the commission of such an offence, a controlled drug is secreted in the person's body.

The term 'relevant offence' means an offence involving a controlled drug under any of the following provisions of the Customs and Excise Management Act 1979:

(a)   Section 50(2) or (3) (importation etc of prohibited goods);

(b)   Section 68(2) (exportation of prohibited goods);

(c)   Section 170(1) (possessing or dealing with prohibited goods);

(d)   Section 170(2) (being concerned in evasion or attempt at evasion of a prohibition).

During this initial period of detention, a detainee under these provisions is obliged by virtue of s 50(2) to:

(a)   provide such specimen of blood or urine for analysis;

(b) submit to such intimate searches, to be carried out by a registered medical practitioner;

(c) submit to such other tests or examinations prescribed by the Secretary of State by regulations made under this paragraph to be carried out by, or under the supervision of, a registered medical practitioner, as the officer may reasonably require, and regulations made under paragraph (c) above shall be made by statutory instrument subject to annulment in pursuance of a resolution of either House of Parliament.

An 'intimate search' is defined in s 50(11) as a search which consists of the physical examination of a person's body orifices. Once the initial period of detention is complete, a person cannot be further detained or obliged to undergo any further tests unless an appropriate warrant is obtained. He may of course be arrested, or detained in pursuance of another enactment, but such steps would take him out of the provisions of the 1987 Act under which further steps by customs officers may be specifically authorised.

Text of s 50(4) of the Criminal Justice (Scotland) Act 1987

4.07   Section 50(4) of the 1987 Act provides:

'Where a person is detained under subsection (1) above and either:

(a) he has failed or refused:
   (i)   to provide a specimen of blood or urine for analysis, or
   (ii) to submit to any search, test or examination referred to in paragraph (b) or (c) or section 50(2) or

(b) as a result of anything done in pursuance of section 50(2) the officer continues to have reasonable grounds for suspecting:
   (i)   that the person has committed or is committing a relevant offence; and
   (ii) that a controlled drug is secreted in the person's body

the procurator fiscal may, at the request of a superior officer apply to the sheriff for a warrant, for the further detention of the person at a customs office or other premises for an additional period of not more than 7 days; and if the sheriff is satisfied that there has been such failure or refusal as is mentioned in paragraph (a) above or, as the case may be, that there are reasonable grounds as mentioned in paragraph (b) above he may grant a warrant for such further detention.'

Comment

4.08   While a warrant granted under s 50(4) is for detention only, it is clear from s 50(8) that the officers may question him in relation to the suspected offence and exercise the same powers of search as are available following an arrest. Section 50(8) also permits the use of reasonable force, except as regards a requirement under s 50(2) to give a specimen of blood or urine, or to submit to intimate searches or other tests.

In all cases, the procurator fiscal will require to satisfy the sheriff that either of the reconditions for grant of the warrant exist and should be prepared to do so both by averment in the application and by amplification at the hearing when the warrant is considered. The section is entirely silent as to whether intimation of the application for the warrant requires to be made to the detainee, a fact all the more surprising because of the provisions of s 49(1) whereby the detainee is entitled to have intimation of his detention and of the place where he is being detained sent to a solicitor.

In Scotland, the only purpose-built detention suite for persons coming within ss 48 and 50 is situated at the office of HM Customs and Excise at Abbotsinch Airport, Glasgow. This unit is used for detainees from all parts of Scotland. The facilities for detention and the standard procedures carried out by customs officers require brief mention, for they are not well publicised. Each detainee is kept in a single cell. Two officers are with him, twenty-four hours a day, and keep a close observation on his movements. The detainee's clothes are removed and he is required to wear a paper suit and carpet slippers. Accordingly, he has no opportunity to conceal anything which may be excreted from his body. His urine samples are analysed with a view to discovering whether anything is concealed in his body. When he requires to defecate, he is obliged to do so at a special toilet facility whereby the faeces are retained and can be examined by customs officers to ascertain whether the detainee has been retaining any prohibited material in his stomach.

The legality of these standard procedures have not, so far as can be ascertained, been challenged in any reported Scottish case. It may be that some of the process is not legally justified, even under a warrant. The warrant is for detention, during which detention *only* the requirements specifically mentioned in s 50 may be made of the detainee. There is nothing specific in that section about the removal of clothes or about compulsion to use special toilet facilities whereby evidence may be obtained. Section 48(6) allows the police to exercise, in the case of a detainee, the same powers of search as are available following an arrest, and this applies to a person detained under a warrant (s 50(8)). Whether the normal powers of search extend to the procedures carried out under a warrant for detention under s 50(4) has not yet been decided.

Style of Application: see Appendix pp 134, 135.

(iii) Criminal Justice (Scotland) Act 1987: drug trafficking

Principal object of warrant: production of material in relation to investigation into drug trafficking.

Background

4.09　Under Part I of the Criminal Justice (Scotland) Act 1987 extensive provisions are made in respect of drug trafficking, which is broadly speaking, doing or being concerned in the following activities:

(a) producing or supplying a controlled drug where the production or supply contravenes s 4(1) of the Misuse of Drugs Act 1971 or a corresponding law;

(b) transporting or storing a controlled drug where possession of the drug contravenes s 5(1) of that Act or a corresponding law; and

(c) importing or exporting a controlled drug where the importation or exportation is prohibited by s 3(1) of that Act or a corresponding law.

As well as dealing with the confiscation of the proceeds of drug trafficking and the enforcement of confiscation orders made under the Act, Part I contains important provisions in respect of investigations into drug trafficking. In particular, s 38 of the 1987 Act gives a sheriff power to make an order for production or access to material which can assist in an investigation, while s 39 covers the granting of search warrants.[1] The two sections are inter-related, in respect that in certain circumstances a warrant under s 39 cannot be granted unless there has been non-compliance with an order granted under s 38.

The relationship between the sections requires close examination.

The procurator fiscal may initiate procedure under s 38(1) by presenting to the sheriff an application for an order in relation to particular material or material of a particular description. If the necessary conditions are satisfied, the sheriff may make an order under s 38(2) that the person who appears to him to be in possession of the material to which the application relates shall:

(a) produce it to a constable or person commissioned by the Commissioners of Customs and Excise for him to take away, or

(b) give a constable or person so commissioned access to it, within such period as the order may specify. This period is normally seven days, unless it appears to the sheriff that a longer or shorter period would be appropriate in the particular circumstances of the application.

The conditions under which such an order may be made are laid out in s 38(4) which is in the following terms:

(a) that there are reasonable grounds for suspecting that a specified person has carried on, or has derived financial or other rewards from, drug trafficking;

(b) that there are reasonable grounds for suspecting that the material to which the application relates:

  (i) is likely to be of substantial value (whether by itself or together with other material) to the investigation for the purpose of which the application is made, and

  (ii) does not consist of or include items subject to legal privilege, and

(c) that there are reasonable grounds for believing that it is in the public interest, having regard:

  (i) to the benefit likely to accrue to the investigation if the material is obtained, and

  (ii) to the circumstances under which the person in possession of the material holds it,

that the material should be produced or that access to it should be given.

Under s 38(5), where the sheriff makes an order that the relevant person should have access to material on any premises, he may also order any person who appears to him to be entitled to grant entry to the premises to allow a constable to enter the premises to obtain access. Provision is also made in relation to information contained in a computer, and for material subject to legal privilege to be exempt from an order made under s 38.

All of the foregoing provisions may be of considerable assistance in a drug trafficking investigation, but only if it is likely that there will be co-operation and compliance by the persons who are made the subject of an order under s 38. Section 39 can however be invoked either where an order under s 38 has been ignored or where the additional terms of s 39 apply.

1   See, generally, 'Tracing Drug Money' 1990 SLT (News) 157.

Text of s 39 of the Criminal Justice (Scotland) Act 1987

4.10   Section 39 of the 1987 Act provides:

'(1) The procurator fiscal may, for the purpose of an investigation into drug trafficking, apply to the sheriff for a warrant under this section in relation to specified premises.

(2) On such application the sheriff may issue a warrant authorising a constable, or person commissioned by the Commissioners of

Customs and Excise, to enter and search the premises if the sheriff is satisfied:

(a) that an order made under section 38 of this Act in relation to material on the premises has not been complied with, or

(b) that the conditions in subsection (3) below are fulfilled, or

(c) that the conditions in subsection (4) below are fulfilled.

(3) The conditions referred to in subsection (2)(b) above are:

(a) that there are reasonable grounds for suspecting that a specified person has carried on, or has derived financial or other rewards from, drug trafficking, and

(b) that the conditions in section 38(4)(b) and (c) of this Act are fulfilled in relation to any material on the premises, and

(c) that it would not be appropriate to make an order under that section in relation to the material because:

    (i) it is not practicable to communicate with any person entitled to produce the material, or

    (ii) it is not practicable to communicate with any person entitled to grant access to the material or entitled to grant entry to the premises on which the material is situated, or

    (iii) the investigation for the purposes of which the application is made might be seriously prejudiced unless a constable or person commissioned as aforesaid could secure immediate access to the material.

(4) The conditions referred to in subsection (2)(c) above are:

(a) that there are reasonable grounds for suspecting that a specified person has carried on, or has derived financial or other rewards from, drug trafficking, and

(b) that there are reasonable grounds for suspecting that there is on the premises material relating to the specified person or to drug trafficking which is likely to be of substantial value (whether by itself or together with other material) to the investigation for the purpose of which the application is made, but that the material cannot at the time of the application be particularised, and

(c) that:

    (i) it is not practicable to communicate with any person entitled to grant entry to the premises, or

    (ii) entry to the premises will not be granted unless a warrant is produced, or

    (iii) the investigation for the purpose of which the application is made might be seriously prejudiced unless a constable or person commissioned as aforesaid arriving at the premises could secure immediate entry to them.

(5) Where a constable or person commissioned as aforesaid has entered premises in the execution of a warrant issued under this

section, he may seize and retain any material, other than items subject to legal privilege, which is likely to be of substantial value (whether by itself or together with other material) to the investigation for the purpose of which the warrant was issued.'

Comment

4.11 It will thus be apparent that the sheriff can issue a warrant under s 39 if any of the alternative situations specified in s 39(2) are satisfied; in particular a warrant can be used to enforce an order already made under s 38. So, the sheriff may not be concerned at the warrant stage with whether the conditions under s 38 still apply, and may only require to be advised that his previous order has not (*semble* for any reason) been complied with. Doubtless this fact will require to be averred in the application and the reason explained when the sheriff is considering it.

Where, alternatively, it is sought to apply immediately for a warrant under s 39(2)(b) or (c), the respective conditions will also require to be averred in the application and expanded on at the hearing, particularly on the issues of public interest and on the inappropriateness of an order under s 38. The emphasis of both subsections is directed to the situation where material of substantial value is thought to be on particular premises, but that material cannot be specified in detail *and* where considerations of practicability, or obstruction, or prejudice arising from delayed entry may be applicable.

Only two terms used in ss 38 and 39 are made the subject of statutory definition in the 1987 Act. Section 40 provides that *'items subject to legal privilege'* means:

(a) communications between a professional legal adviser and his client or

(b) communication made in connection with or in contemplation of legal proceedings and for the purposes of these proceedings, being communications which would in legal proceedings be protected from disclosure by virtue of any rule of law relating to the confidentiality of communications;

while the term *'premises'* is defined as including any place and in particular:

(a) any vehicle, vessel, aircraft or hovercraft;

(b) any offshore installation within the meaning of s 1 of the Mineral Workings (Offshore Installations) Act 1971 and

(c) any tent or moveable structure.

Beyond this, no guidance is given by statute to the interpretation of terms such as 'financial or other rewards' from drug trafficking;

'substantial value' to an investigation, or indeed the key word 'material' for which a search may be ordered. All this is left to the sheriff; so far, there have been no reported cases in Scotland where such terminology has been explored.[1]

Style of Application: see Appendix pp 136, 137

1   The extent of legal privilege under equivalent English legislation was considered by the House of Lords in *R v Central Criminal Court ex parte Francis and Francis* [1989] AC 346, where the issue was whether a client's documents in the hands of a firm of solicitors could be the subject of an inspection order. It was held that items otherwise within legal privilege were not in fact within the privilege where they were held with the intention of furthering a criminal purpose, whether the intention was that of the holder or any other person. See also *R v Guildhall Magistrates Court ex parte Primlaks Holdings Co (Panama) Inc* [1989] 2 WLR 841.

(iv) Criminal Justice (Scotland) Act 1987: serious fraud

Principal object of warrant: entry/search of premises for documents in cases of serious fraud where voluntary production is not made in response to notice to produce, or where notice is not served.

Background

4.12   Sections 51–54 of the Criminal Justice (Scotland) Act 1987 make detailed provision for the investigation of serious or complex fraud. The statutory powers under ss 52–54 are triggered by the giving of a direction under s 51 by the Lord Advocate; he may do so under that section where it appears to him that a suspected offence may involve a fraud of that nature and that there is good reason to give such a direction for the purpose of investigating the affairs or any aspect of the affairs of any person. In terms of such a direction a nominated officer (other than a constable) is entitled to exercise powers of investigation either generally or in respect of a particular case.

Under s 52(1) and (2) a nominated officer may make require-ments of certain persons to attend before him and give information and also to produce documents relevant to the investigation, all following service of a notice in writing.

By s 52(8) the term 'documents' in the section includes informa-tion recorded in any form and, in relation to information recorded otherwise than in legible form, references to its production include references to producing a copy of the information in legible form.

Text of s 52(3) of the Criminal Justice (Scotland) Act 1987

4.13   Section 52(3) of the 1987 Act provides:

'(3) Where, on a petition presented by the procurator fiscal, the sheriff is satisfied, in relation to any documents, that there are reasonable grounds for believing:

(a) that:

    (i) a person has failed to comply with an obligation under this section to produce them;

    (ii) it is not practicable to serve a notice under s 52(2) in relation to them; or

    (iii) the service of such a notice in relation to them might seriously prejudice the investigation; and

(b) that they are on premises specified in the petition,

he may issue such a warrant as is mentioned in s 52(4)...'

The latter provides that the warrant to be issued is a warrant authorising a constable together with any other persons named in the warrant:

'(a) to enter (using such force as is reasonably necessary for the purpose) and search the premises; and

(b) to take possession of any documents appearing to be documents of the description specified in the petition or to take in relation to any documents so appearing any other steps which may appear to be necessary for preserving them and preventing interference with them.'

Comment

4.14   There is now a separate department at the Crown Office in Edinburgh which deals with all cases of serious fraud reported to it by regional procurators fiscal. Investigations are carried out by staff specially trained for this purpose, who are also responsible for conducting any resultant prosecutions.

It is a specific offence for a person, knowing or suspecting that an investigation under s 52 of the 1987 Act is being carried out or is likely to be carried out, to falsify, conceal, destroy or otherwise dispose of, or to cause or permit the falsification, concealment, destruction or disposal of documents which he knows or suspects or has reasonable grounds to suspect are or would be relevant to such an investigation.[1]

Style of Application: see Appendix p 138.

1   Criminal Justice (Scotland) Act 1987, s 53(1).

(v) Explosives Act 1875

Principal objects of warrant: entry to premises; search for explosives and to take samples thereof.

Background

4.15   The Explosives Act 1875 regulates the manufacture of explosives and the places where they may be kept, all with a view to promoting public safety. But most criminal offences in connection with explosives are to be found in the Explosive Substances Act 1883, which renders criminal *inter alia* the causing of explosions (s 2); the doing of acts with intent to cause by an explosive substance an explosion likely to endanger life or property (s 3); and possession of explosives under such circumstances as to give rise to a reasonable suspicion that the possessor does not have them in his possession or under his control for a lawful object (s 4). Sections 73 and 74 of the 1875 Act contain powers to search for explosives; by s 8(1) of the 1883 Act these sections apply in like manner as if a crime under the 1883 Act were an offence under the 1875 Act. Section 73 gives power to issue a warrant.

Text of s 73 of the Explosives Act 1875

4.16   Section 73 of the 1875 Act provides:
'Where any of the following officers, – namely, any Government inspector, or any constable or any officer of the local authority, if such constable or officer is specially authorised either (a) by a warrant of a justice (which warrant such justice may grant upon reasonable ground being assigned on oath), or (b) (where it appears to a superintendent or other officer of police of equal or superior rank, or to a Government inspector, that the case is one of emergency and that the delay in obtaining a warrant would be likely to endanger life,) by a written order from such superintendent, officer, or inspector, – has reasonable cause to believe that any offence has been or is being committed with respect to an explosive in any place (whether a building or not, or a carriage, boat, or ship), or that any explosive is in any such place in contravention of this Act, or that the provisions of this Act are not duly observed in any such place, such officer may, on producing, if demanded, in the case of a Government inspector a copy of his appointment, and in the case of any other officer his authority, enter at any time, and if needs be by force, and as well on Sunday as on other days, the said place, and every part thereof, and examine the same, and search for explosives therein, and take

samples of any explosive and ingredient of an explosive therein, and any substance reasonably supposed to be an explosive, or such ingredient which may be found therein.'

Comment

4.17 Our Victorian forefathers clearly thought it necessary to legislate specifically to the effect that a warrant under s 73 could be executed on a Sunday as well as on other days; such a provision is not encountered in more modern legislation on warrants. Section 73 goes on to make it a specific offence for a person to fail to admit into any place occupied by him any officer demanding entrance in pursuance of the section, or to obstruct him in any way in the execution of his duty.

Section 73 restricts the granting of a warrant to a justice of the peace: the extended meaning of 'justice' as including the sheriff appears to be of no application.[1]

Style of Application: see Appendix p 139.

1   See Criminal Procedure (Scotland) Act 1975, s 462

(vi) Firearms Act 1968

Principal objects of warrant: entry to premises; search of persons and seizure of firearms or ammunition.

Background

4.18 Part I of the Firearms Act 1968 (as amended) makes detailed provision as to the possession, handling and distribution of weapons and ammunition; the prevention of crime; and the protection of public safety. The Act contains various offences; some of those which are commonly encountered in practice are possession of a sawn-off shotgun (s 4); possession of a firearm with intent to cause injury (s 16); carrying a firearm in a public place without lawful authority or reasonable excuse (s 19); and possession of firearms by persons previously convicted of crime (s 21).

Section 46(1) makes provision for the granting of a warrant in respect of a 'relevant offence'. By s 46(2) of the Act it is provided that the offences relevant for the purposes of s 46(1) are all offences under the Act except an offence under s 22(3) (which relates to possession of an assembled shotgun by a person under fifteen years of age while not under supervision of an adult or where the shotgun is not securely covered) or an offence relating specifically to air weapons.

It should also be noted that generally the provisions of the 1968 Act are applied by virtue of the Firearms Act 1982 to any imitation firearm which has the appearance of being a firearm to which s 1 of the 1968 Act applies. Certain alterations to the law on firearms were also made by the Firearms (Amendment) Act 1989. From the standpoint of the law on warrants however, the magistrate or sheriff dealing with an application will of course require to be satisfied that the offence suspected relates to a firearm within the meaning of the statutes.

Text of s 46(1) of the Firearms Act 1968

4.19   Section 46(1) of the 1968 Act provides:

'(1) If a justice of the peace or, in Scotland, the sheriff . . . is satisfied by information on oath that there is reasonable ground for suspecting that an offence relevant for the purposes of this section has been, is being, or is about to be committed, he may grant a search warrant authorising a constable named therein:

(a) to enter at any time any premises or place named in the warrant, if necessary by force, and to search the premises or place and every person found there;

(b) to seize and detain any firearm or ammunition which he may find on the premises or place, or on any such person, in respect of which or in connection with which he has reasonable ground for suspecting that an offence relevant for the purposes of this section has been, is being or is about to be committed; and

(c) if the premises are those of a registered firearms dealer, to examine any books relating to the business.'

Comment

4.20   In *Innes v Jessop*[1] police carried out a search by virtue of a warrant under the 1968 Act for firearms and ammunition. However a driving licence and a tax exemption certificate (subsequently discovered to have been stolen) and other articles unconnected with firearms were taken away by the police. The accused was convicted of the reset of the licence and the certificate, but the conviction was quashed on the basis that these items were not covered by the warrant and that the circumstances of their removal carried the implication that the search was a random one.

Style of Application: see Appendix p 140.

1   1989 SCCR 441.

(vii) Food Safety Act 1990

Principal objects of warrant: entry to premises; inspection of records and equipment.

Background

4.21   The Food Safety Act 1990 makes new provisions regulating the manufacture and sale of food and drink throughout the United Kingdom. The Food and Drugs (Scotland) Act 1956 has been repealed, but there continue to exist various powers of entry (with or without a warrant) conferred upon appropriate officials charged with the duty of enforcing the legislation. The principal offence under s 8 of the 1990 Act is that of supplying food that does not comply with food safety requirements, a provision designed to cover food which is injurious to health, unfit for human consumption or is contaminated. The relative provisions of the 1990 Act came into force on 1 January 1991.

Under s 32(1) of the 1990 Act an authorised officer of an enforcement authority enjoys certain rights of entry to premises at all reasonable hours on production of a duly authenticated document showing his authority. He may:

(a)   enter any premises within the authority's area for the purpose of ascertaining whether there is or has been on the premises any contravention of the provisions of the Act, or of regulations or orders made under it;

(b)   enter any business premises, whether within or outside the authority's area, for the purpose of ascertaining whether there is on the premises any evidence of any contravention within that area of any such provisions; and

(c)   in the case of an authorised officer of a food authority, enter any premises for the purpose of the performance by the authority of their functions under the Act.

He can however enter a private dwelling house only after giving twenty-four hours notice to the occupier of the intended entry. So far as Scotland is concerned, the Act provides (ss 5 and 6) generally that enforcement of the Act is to be carried out by 'food authorities', namely the District or Islands Councils.

Text of s 32(2) of the Food Safety Act 1990

4.22   Section 32(2) of the 1990 Act provides:

'If a justice of the peace, on sworn information in writing, is satisfied that there is reasonable ground for entry into any premises for any such purpose as is mentioned in sub-section (1) and *either*:

(a) admission to the premises has been refused, or a refusal is apprehended, and that notice of the intention to apply for a warrant has been given to the occupier; or

(b) that an application for admission, or the giving of such a notice, would defeat the object of the entry, or that the case is one of urgency, or that the premises are unoccupied or the occupier temporarily absent

the justice may by warrant signed by him authorise the authorised officer to enter the premises, if need be by reasonable force.'

Comment

4.23   So far as Scotland is concerned, the term 'justice of the peace' includes a sheriff and a magistrate (s 32(9)). A warrant granted under s 32 continues in force for one month (s 32(3)). Various other provisions govern the carrying out of the functions of the authorised officer. By s 32(4) of the 1990 Act, an authorised officer entering any premises (whether with or without a warrant) may take with him such other persons as he considers necessary, and on leaving any unoccupied premises which he has entered by virtue of a warrant, must leave them as effectively secured against unauthorised entry as he found them. On entering premises (again with or without a warrant) an authorised officer may inspect any records (in whatever form they are held) relating to a food business and, where any such records are kept by means of a computer:

(a) may have access to, and inspect and check the operation of, any computer and any associated apparatus or material which is or has been in use in connection with the records; and

(b) may require any person having charge of, or otherwise concerned with the operation of, the computer, apparatus or material to afford him such assistance as he may reasonably require.

In particular, any officer exercising any such powers of inspection and access to equipment following entry to premises may:

(a) seize and detain any records which he has reason to believe may be required as evidence in proceedings under any of the provisions of the Act or of regulations or orders made under it; and

(b) where the records are kept by means of a computer, may require the records to be produced in a form in which they may be taken away.

It is a specific offence intentionally to obstruct any person acting in the execution of the Act,[1] which would clearly include the obstruction of an authorised officer seeking to execute a warrant.

Style of Application: see Appendix p 141.

1   Food Safety Act 1990, s 33(1).

(viii) Misuse of Drugs Act 1971

Principal object of warrant: entry and search of premises and persons therein for controlled drugs and documents relating to drugs transactions.

Background

4.24   One of the commonest situations in which a justice of the peace or sheriff will require to consider an application for a warrant is where it is intended to invoke the provisions of the Misuse of Drugs Act 1971, which contains a number of important and frequently committed offences in connection with controlled drugs. Such drugs are classified according to their noxious properties and the degree of harm they are liable to cause; Sch 2 of the Act provides the relative listings. The principal offences under the Act are those created by ss 4 (unlawful production and supply), 5 (unlawful possession and possession with intent to supply) and 8 (permitting the use of premises for certain activities in regard to controlled drugs). In addition, by s 3, importation or exportation of controlled drugs is prohibited, although offences in relation to this activity are prosecuted not under the 1971 Act, but under the Customs and Excise Management Act 1979.

The 1971 Act contains various powers of enforcement, including 'stop and search' by the police and entry to premises. Power to act under warrant is governed by s 23(3).

Text of s 23(3) of the Misuse of Drugs Act 1971

4.25   Section 23(3) of the 1971 Act provides:

'(3) If . . . a justice of the peace, a magistrate or a sheriff is satisfied by information on oath that there is reasonable ground for suspecting:

(a)   that any controlled drugs are, in contravention of this Act or of any regulation made thereunder, in the possession of a person on any premises; or

(b)   that a document directly or indirectly relating to, or connected with, a transaction or dealing which has, or an intended transaction or dealing which would if carried out be, an offence under this Act, or in the case of a transaction or dealing carried out or intended to be carried out in a place outside the United Kingdom, an offence against the provision of a corresponding law in force in that place, is in the possession of person on any premises, he may grant a warrant authorising any constable acting for the police area in which the premises are situated at any time or times within one month from the date of the warrant, to enter, if need be by force, the premises named in the warrant, and to search the premises and any persons found therein and, if there is reasonable ground for suspecting that an offence under this Act has been committed in relation to any controlled drugs found on the premises or in the possession of any such persons, or that a document so found is such a document as is mentioned in paragraph (b) above, to seize and detain those drugs or that document, as the case may be.'

Comment

4.26 Section 23(3) is frequently invoked in practice, so inevitably the terms of the section have come under close judicial scrutiny from time to time. This has arisen both at the stage of presentation of an application for a warrant and also later, when the admissibility in evidence of the fruits of a search carried out under warrant is challenged at trial.

At the outset, it is thought that any police officer giving information on oath in support of an application ought to be in a position to specify what drug he has reasonable ground for suspecting is in the possession of the person or on the premises concerned, at least for the purpose of satisfying the court that it is 'controlled' within the meaning of the Act. Further, the application must be specific as to the address of the premises to be searched, since failure to give this detail will be fatal to the legality of the warrant. In *HM Advocate v Cumming*[1] the omission to state the address was held not to be excusable by the urgency of the need to search and the haste involved. The court observed:

'Urgency may well excuse a search without any warrant in very special circumstances but once a warrant had been obtained I can see no reason why proper care should not have been taken to complete the warrant in proper form. The officers from the Scottish Crime Squad who undertook the search would, I have no doubt, have been well acquainted with the formalities attending a search. I would respectfully agree with the observations of the

Lord Justice-General (Cooper) in *McGovern v HM Advocate* 1950 JC 33 at 37. Unless the principles under which police investigations are carried out are adhered to with reasonable strictness, the anchor of the entire system for the protection of the public will very soon begin to drag'.[2]

But the address of the premises need not be given in the body of the warrant itself, provided it can be readily ascertained. In *Bell v HM Advocate*[3] an objection was taken to evidence obtained under a drugs warrant which consisted of one sheet of paper at the top of which was set out information on oath by a constable that there were grounds for suspecting the presence of drugs in specified premises. The rest of the document set out the warrant which authorised search of the 'said premises'. The trial judge repelled an objection to the admissibility of the evidence of what was found; this decision was upheld on appeal when it was stated that the test was whether the owner of premises to whom a warrant was shown would be able to satisfy himself that the warrant clearly identified the premises concerned.

A person who comes to the door of premises to be searched under a warrant, while holding a cigarette suspected of containing cannabis, comes within the category of 'any person found' on the premises and may be searched under the warrant.[4] A doorstep is part of a house for the purposes of a search of premises under a drugs warrant.[5] Great care must be taken in relation to premises containing separately-occupied rooms, for they are not necessarily analogous to a 'family home.'[6]

A warrant proceeding on information that drugs 'and/or' documents are suspected to be present in premises is not void from uncertainty.[7]

A drugs warrant which is unsigned will be invalid,[8] as will a warrant which is undated, in view of the time limit on execution in s 23(3).[9]

Style of Application: see Appendix p 142.

1   1983 SCCR 15
2   Ibid at p 19
3   1988 SCCR 292
4   *McCarron v Allan* 1988 SCCR 9
5   *Guthrie v Hamilton* 1988 SCCR 330, 1988 SLT 823
6   *McAvoy v Jessop* 1988 SCCR 172
7   *Baird v HM Advocate* 1989 SCCR 55
8   *HM Advocate v Bell* 1984 SCCR 430
9   *Bulloch v HM Advocate* 1980 SLT (Notes) 5; *HM Advocate v Welsh* 1987 SCCR 647

(ix) The Prevention of Terrorism (Temporary Provisions) Act 1989

Principal objects of warrants: search for, and arrest of a person suspected of terrorist acts, or subject to exclusion order; search for material to be used in terrorist investigation.

(a) *Persons: search and arrest*

Background: section 15 warrants

4.27 The Prevention of Terrorism (Temporary Provisions) Act 1989 makes a number of important provisions relating to the detection, prevention and prosecution of terrorist offences. At present the Act lasts for a period of one year only, but may be (and is) renewed annually by Parliament. Section 14(1)(b) of the Act permits a constable to arrest without warrant a person whom he has reasonable grounds for suspecting to be a person who is or has been concerned in the commission, preparation or instigation of acts of terrorism, such acts being connected with the affairs of Northern Ireland or acts of terrorism of any other description except acts connected solely with the affairs of the United Kingdom or any part of the United Kingdom other than Northern Ireland. 'Terrorism' is defined as 'the use of violence for political ends, and includes any use of violence for the purpose of putting the public or any section of the public in fear'. Power to grant warrants is contained in s 15.

Text of s 15 of the Prevention of Terrorism (Temporary Provisions) Act 1989

4.28 Section 15 of the 1989 Act provides:

'(1) If a justice of the peace is satisfied that there are reasonable grounds for suspecting that a person whom a constable believes to be liable to arrest under s 14(1)(b) above is to be found on any premises he may grant a search warrant authorising any constable to enter those premises for the purpose of searching for and arresting that person.

(2) In Scotland the power to issue a warrant under subsection (1) above shall be exercised by a sheriff or a justice of the peace, an application for such a warrant shall be supported by evidence on oath and a warrant shall not authorise a constable to enter any premises unless he is a constable for the police area in which they are situated.'

Background: Schedule 2 cases

4.29   Schedule 2 of the 1989 Act sets out, *inter alia* certain procedures in connection with an exclusion order made by the Secretary of State under ss 5, 6 or 7 of the Act. A person subject to an exclusion order may be removed from the relevant territory pursuant to removal directions by the Secretary of State; and he may be detained pending the giving of such direction. Under para 7(2) of Sch 2 to the Act, such a person is liable to arrest without warrant by any person within the definition of 'examining officer', which broadly speaking includes a police constable, and certain immigration officers and officers of HM Customs and Excise. Power to grant warrants is contained in para 8 of Sch 2.

Text of Schedule 2, para 8 of the Prevention of Terrorism (Temporary Provisions) Act 1989

4.30   Schedule 2, para 8 of the 1989 Act provides:

'(1) If a justice of the peace is satisfied that there are reasonable grounds for suspecting that a person liable to be arrested under paragraph 7(2) above is to be found on any premises he may grant a search warrant authorising any constable to enter those premises for the purpose of searching for and arresting that person.

(2) In Scotland the power to issue a warrant under sub-paragraph (1) above shall be exercised by a sheriff or a justice of the peace, an application for such a warrant shall be supported by evidence on oath and a warrant shall not authorise a constable to enter any premises unless he is a constable for the police area in which they are situated.'

Background: Schedule 5 cases

4.31   Schedule 5 of the Act makes provision for the examination of persons arriving in or seeking to leave Great Britain or Northern Ireland by ship or aircraft for the purposes of determining whether that person appears to be a person who is or has been concerned in the commission, preparation or instigation of certain acts of terrorism; or whether any such person is subject to an exclusion order; or has contravened s 8 of the Act, which creates certain offences in connection with exclusion orders. Again, a person who is examined under Sch 5 may be detained pending conclusion of his examination or other decisions about his future. Under para 6(4) of Sch 5 he may be arrested without warrant by an examining officer. Paragraph 7 of the Schedule allows for the granting of a warrant.

Text of Schedule 5, para 7 of the Prevention of Terrorism (Temporary Provisions) Act 1989

4.32   Schedule 5, para 7 of the 1989 Act provides:

'(1) If a justice of the peace is satisfied that there are reasonable grounds for suspecting that a person liable to be arrested under para 6(4) above is to be found on any premises he may grant a search warrant authorising any constable to enter those premises for the purpose of searching for and arresting that person.

(2) In Scotland the power to issue a warrant under sub-para (1) above shall be exercised by a sheriff or a justice of the peace, an application for such a warrant shall be supported by evidence on oath and a warrant shall not authorise a constable to enter any premises unless he is a constable for the police area in which they are situated.'

Comment

4.33   As will be observed, every application for a warrant under s 15, Sch 2 or Sch 5 must be supported by evidence on oath. Throughout the Act, the term 'premises' includes any place and in particular includes (a) any vehicle, vessel or aircraft, (b) any offshore installation as defined in s 1 of the Mineral Workings (Offshore Installations) Act 1971; and (c) any tent or moveable structure. In executing a warrant, a constable may, if necessary, use reasonable force for the purpose of exercising any powers conferred on him under or by virtue of the Act, but this is without prejudice to any provision of the Act or of any instrument made under it, which implies that a person may use reasonable force in connection with that provision.

(b) *Production of material*

Background: Schedule 7 warrants

4.34   Part II of Sch 7 of the 1989 Act contains a number of important provisions regarding production of material and warrants to search. The procurator fiscal may make certain applications to the sheriff for the purpose of a terrorist investigation, which is defined as covering a broad range of enquiry into the commission, preparation or instigation of acts of terrorism, acts done in furtherance or in connection therewith, the resources of proscribed organisations and whether there are grounds for proscribing further bodies. Initially the procurator fiscal may proceed under para 12 of Sch 7 by seeking an order by the sheriff for the production of particular material or material of a particular description, either to a constable to take away or by giving a constable access to it. Such an order is however only competent if the conditions set out in para 12(5) are met: these are (a) that a terrorist investigation is being carried out and that there are reasonable grounds for believing that the material to which the application relates is likely to be of substantial value (whether by itself or together with other material) to the investigation and (b) that there are reasonable grounds for believing that it is in the public interest, having regard (i) to the benefit likely to accrue to the investigation if the material is obtained and (ii) to the circumstances under which the person in possession of the material holds it, that the material should be produced or that access to it should be given. There are detailed provisions in para 12 as to material stored on computer and the restricted extent of the obligation of secrecy.

In the event that an order under para 12 has not been complied with, or alternatively that certain conditions are met, the sheriff may issue a warrant under para 14.

Text of Schedule 7, para 14 of the Prevention of Terrorism (Temporary Provisions) Act 1989

4.35   Schedule 7, para 14 of the 1989 Act provides:

'(1) A procurator fiscal may, for the purpose of a terrorist investigation, apply to a sheriff for a warrant under this paragraph in relation to specified premises.

(2) On such application the sheriff may issue a warrant authorising a constable to enter and search the premises if the sheriff is satisfied–
(a) that an order made under paragraph 12 above in relation to material on the premises has not been complied with; or
(b) that the conditions in sub-paragraph (3) below are fulfilled.

(3) The conditions referred to in sub-paragraph (2)(b) above are–
(a) that there are reasonable grounds for believing that there is material on the premises specified in the application in respect of which the conditions in sub-paragraph (5) of paragraph 12 above are fulfilled; and
(b) that it would not be appropriate to make an order under that paragraph in relation to the material because–
   (i) it is not practicable to communicate with any person entitled to produce the material; or
   (ii) it is not practicable to communicate with any person entitled to grant access to the material or entitled to grant entry to the premises on which the material is situated; or

(iii) the investigation for the purposes of which the application is made may be seriously prejudiced unless a constable can secure immediate access to the material.

(4) A warrant under this paragraph shall authorise a constable to enter the premises specified in the warrant and to search the premises and any persons found there and to seize and retain any material found there or on any such person, if he has reasonable grounds for believing that it is likely to be of substantial value (whether by itself or together with other material) to the investigation for the purpose of which the warrant was issued.

(5) A warrant under this paragraph may authorise persons named in the warrant to accompany a constable who is executing it.'

Comment

4.36   As well as the above powers to obtain a warrant, provision is also made under para 15 of the Schedule for an order by the sheriff on any person specified in the order to provide an explanation of any material seized in pursuance of a warrant under para 14.

Schedule 7 of the 1989 Act also contains a set of provisions which deal with urgent cases. If a police officer of at least the rank of superintendent has reasonable grounds for believing that the case is one of great emergency and that in the interests of the State immediate action is necessary, he may by a written order signed by him give to any constable the authority which may be given by a search warrant under para 14. Where such an authority is given, particulars of the case must be notified as soon as may be to the Secretary of State. Again, in such a case an explanation of seized materials may be required; failure to comply is, in these cases, a criminal offence.

The whole of Part II of Sch 7 is without prejudice to (a) any power of entry or search or any power to seize or retain property which is otherwise exercisable by a constable; and (b) any rule of law whereby (i) communication between a professional legal adviser and his client, or (ii) communication made in connection with or in contemplation of legal proceedings and for the purposes of those proceedings, are in legal proceedings protected from disclosure on the ground of confidentiality. A constable acting on a warrant under para 14 may, if necessary, open lockfast places on premises specified in the warrant. A search of any person may only be carried out by a person of the same sex.

Application under s 15: see Appendix p 143.

(x) Salmon and Freshwater Fisheries (Protection) (Scotland) Act 1951

Principal objects of warrant: entry to premises and vehicles for the purpose of detecting offences under the Act; search of persons.

Background

4.37 The Salmon and Freshwater Fisheries (Protection) (Scotland) Act 1951 contains a number of provisions prohibiting certain methods of taking and destroying fish. Section 1 covers the poaching of salmon, while s 2 prohibits fishing for salmon in any inland water except by means of rod and line or by net and coble. Fishing for other freshwater fish except by rod and line is prohibited, with certain exceptions, by the provisions of s 2. Section 3 prohibits illegal fishing by two or more persons acting together, while s 4 prohibits the using of explosive and other noxious substances for the destruction of fish. The enforcement of these and other provisions of the Act is carried out by water bailiffs appointed by the relative district board, although police constables and other persons authorised by the Secretary of State are also empowered to act. All such persons enjoy under s 10 of the Act statutory powers of examination, search and seizure of boats and equipment. These powers are exercisable without warrant, but in certain circumstances a warrant can be obtained.

Text of s 11 of the Salmon and Freshwater Fisheries (Protection) (Scotland) Act 1951

4.38 Section 11 of the 1951 Act provides:
'(1) A sheriff or any justice of the peace, if satisfied by information on oath that there is reasonable ground to suspect any offence against any of the provisions of sections three and four of this Act to have been committed and that evidence of the commission of the offence is to be found on any premises or in any vehicle, may grant a warrant authorising any water bailiff, constable or person appointed by the Secretary of State in pursuance of the last foregoing section at any time or times within one week from the date thereof to enter, if necessary by force, the said premises and every part thereof or the said vehicle for the purposes of detecting the offence.

(2) A person authorised by any such warrant as aforesaid to search any premises or any vehicle may search every person who is found in, or whom he has reasonable ground to believe to have recently left or to be about to enter, those premises or that vehicle, as the case may be.'

Comment

4.39   A constable (but not a water bailiff or other authorised person) has power to search a vehicle and a person who is found therein, or whom he has reasonable grounds to believe to have recently left or to be about to enter the vehicle, in situations where by reason of urgency or other good cause it is impracticable to apply for a warrant. This power under s 11(3) of the Act exists only where a constable has reasonable grounds for suspecting that an offence against any of the provisions of ss 3 or 4 of the Act has been committed.

Style of Application: see Appendix p 144

(xi) Taxes Management Act 1970

Principal object of warrant: entry and search of premises

Background

4.40   The Taxes Management Act 1970 (as amended) makes extensive provision for the administration, assessment and collection of income tax, corporation tax and capital gains tax under the care and management of the Commissioners of Inland Revenue (known as 'the Board'). Part III of the Act contains a group of provisions dealing with the making of returns and the provision of information. Section 20 of the Act gives a tax inspector and the Board power to call for delivery of documents in the possession of the taxpayer or others which contain or may contain information relevant to a person's tax liability. The present law on entry to premises by means of a warrant is contained in s 20c of the Act.

Text of s 20c of the Taxes Management Act 1970

4.41   Section 20c of the 1970 Act provides:
   '(1) If the appropriate judicial authority is satisfied on information on oath given by an officer of the Board that–
(a)   there is reasonable ground for suspecting that an offence involving serious fraud in connection with, or in relation to, tax is being, has been or is about to be committed and that evidence of it is to be found on premises specified in the information; and
(b)   in applying under this section, the officer acts with the approval of the Board given in relation to the particular case,
the authority may issue a warrant in writing authorising an officer of the Board to enter the premises, if necessary by force, at any time

within 14 days from the time of issue of the warrant, and search them.

(1A) Without prejudice to the generality of the concept of serious fraud—

(a) any offence which involves fraud is for the purposes of this section an offence involving serious fraud if its commission had led, or is intended or likely to lead, either to substantial financial gain to any person or to serious prejudice to the proper assessment or collection of tax; and

(b) an offence which, if considered alone, would not be regarded as involving serious fraud may nevertheless be so regarded if there is reasonable ground for suspecting that it forms part of a course of conduct which is, or but for its detection would be, likely to result in serious prejudice to the proper assessment or collection of tax.

(1B) The powers conferred by a warrant under this section shall not be exercisable—

(a) by more than such number of officers of the Board as may be specified in the warrant;

(b) outside such times of day as may be so specified;

(c) if the warrant so provides, otherwise than in the presence of a constable in uniform.

(2) Section 4A of the Inland Revenue Regulation Act 1890 (Board's functions to be exercisable by an officer acting under their authority) does not apply to the giving of Board approval under this section.

(3) An officer who enters the premises under the authority of a warrant under this section may—

(a) take with him such other persons as appear to him to be necessary;

(b) seize and remove any things whatsoever found there which he has reasonable cause to believe may be required as evidence for the purposes of proceedings in respect of such an offence as is mentioned in subsection (1) above; and

(c) search or cause to be searched any person found on the premises whom he has reasonable cause to believe to be in possession of any such things;

but no person shall be searched except by a person of the same sex.

(4) Nothing in subsection (3) above authorises the seizure and removal of documents in the possession of a barrister, advocate or solicitor with respect to which a claim to professional privilege could be maintained.

(5) An officer of the Board seeking to exercise the powers conferred by a warrant under this section or, if there is more than one such officer, that one of them who is in charge of the search—

(a) if the occupier of the premises concerned is present at the time the search is to begin, shall supply a copy of the warrant endorsed with his name to the occupier;
(b) if at that time the occupier is not present but a person who appears to the officer to be in charge of the premises is present, shall supply such a copy to that person; and
(c) if neither paragraph (a) nor paragraph (b) above applies, shall leave such a copy in a prominent place on the premises.

(6) Where entry to premises has been made with a warrant under this section, and the officer making the entry has seized any things under the authority of the warrant, he shall endorse on or attach to the warrant a list of the things seized.'

Comment

4.42   In Scotland the 'appropriate judicial authority' is the sheriff.[1] The term 'document' has the same meaning as it has in Part III of the Law Reform (Miscellaneous Provisions) (Scotland) Act 1968:[2] it therefore includes, in addition to a document in writing, (a) any map, plan, graph or drawing; (b) any photograph; (c) any disc, tape, sound track or other device in which sounds or other data (not being visual images) are embodied so as to be capable (with or without the aid of some other equipment) of being reproduced therefrom; and (d) any film, negative, tape or other device in which one or more visual images are embodied so as to be capable (as aforesaid) of being reproduced therefrom.

The provisions of s 20C are extremely formal on the question of supply of information to the occupier, as are the provisions of s 20CC as to the procedure where documents are removed. They are consistent with the general English (but not Scottish) law on how searches must be carried out, on which see the Police and Criminal Evidence Act 1984, Part II and relative codes of practice.

The status of a notice under s 20(3) of the Taxes Management Act 1970 is the same as search warrant at common law or under the Misuse of Drugs Act 1971: the notice can be spoken to by an investigator to demonstrate that the appropriate procedure has been carried out and no further proof of the validity of the notice is required.[3]

Style of Application: see Appendix p 145.

1   Taxes Management Act 1970, s 20D(1)
2   Ibid, s 20D(3)
3   *Boyle v HM Advocate* 1990 SCCR 480

(xii) Trade Descriptions Act 1968

Principal object of warrant: entry to premises for the purposes of exercising powers under the Act to inspect and seize goods and documents, where admission to premises cannot be obtained by other means or is inappropriate.

Background

4.43 The Trade Descriptions Act 1968 contains a number of offences in connection with false trade descriptions applied to goods, the making of false representations as to supply of goods or services and the making of false or misleading statements as to services in the course of a trade or business. Enforcement of the Act is in the hands of the local weights and measures authority, this being in Scotland the Regional or Islands Council. An authorised officer of the weights and measures authority (or a Government department) has extensive powers under s 28 of the Act, including the inspection of premises, requiring the production of books and documents where he has reasonable cause to suspect that an offence under the Act has been committed, and the seizure of goods for testing or as evidence of an offence. Section 28 also contains power to apply for a warrant.

Text of s 28(3) and (4) of the Trade Descriptions Act 1968

4.44 Section 28(3) and (4) of the 1968 Act provides:
    '(3) If a justice of the peace, on sworn information in writing–
(a) is satisfied that there is reasonable grounds to believe either–
    (i) that any goods, books or documents which a duly authorised officer has power under this section to inspect are on any premises and that their inspection is likely to disclose evidence of the commission of an offence under this Act; or
    (ii) that any offence under this Act has been, is being or is about to be committed on any premises; and
(b) is also satisfied either–
    (i) that admission to the premises has been or is likely to be refused and that notice of intention to apply for a warrant under this subsection has been given to the occupier; or
    (ii) that an application for admission, or the giving of such a notice, would defeat the object of the entry or that the premises are unoccupied or that the occupier is temporarily absent and it might defeat the object of the entry to await his return
the justice may by warrant under his hand, which shall continue in

force for a period of one month, authorise an officer of a local weights and measures authority or of a Government department to enter the premises, if need be by force.

In the application of this subsection to Scotland, 'justice of the peace' shall be construed as including a sheriff and a magistrate.

(4) An officer entering any premises by virtue of this section may take with him such other persons and such equipment as may appear to him necessary; and on leaving any premises which he has entered by virtue of a warrant under the preceding subsection he shall, if the premises are unoccupied or the occupier is temporarily absent, leave them effectively secured against trespassers as he found them.'

Comment

4.45   It will be observed that the sheriff or justice of the peace must be satisfied of the matters mentioned both in sub-para (a) and (b) of sub-s (3). The term 'premises' includes any place and any stall, vehicle, ship or aircraft.[1] Under s 28(1) an officer has certain powers of entry to premises without warrant, but this excludes premises used only as a dwelling. But the latter can still be premises for the other purposes of the Act, and so if goods, books or documents were taken to a private residence, s 28(3) would probably apply to premises used in this manner.

Style of Application: see Appendix p 146.

1   Trade Descriptions Act 1968, s 39

(xiii) Value Added Tax Act 1983

Principal objects of warrant: entry to premises; search of persons; seizure and removal of documents or other things required as evidence of an offence under the Act.

Background

4.46   The Value Added Tax Act 1983 consolidates the law on VAT. Section 38 provides that Sch 7 of the Act has effect with respect to administration, collection and enforcement of the tax; the relative duties are carried out by officers of HM Customs and Excise. Under para 10(1) and (2) of Schedule 7, an authorised officer has certain powers of entry to business premises, inspection of those premises and any goods found on them. A warrant may be granted under para 10(3).

Text of Sch 7, para 10(3) of the Value Added Tax Act 1983

4.47   Schedule 7 para 10(3) of the 1983 Act provides:

'(3) If a justice of the peace or in Scotland a justice (within the meaning of section 462 of the Criminal Procedure (Scotland) Act 1975) is satisfied on information on oath that there is reasonable ground for suspecting that an offence in connection with the tax is being, has been or is about to be committed on any premises or that evidence of the commission of such an offence is to be found there, he may issue a warrant in writing authorising any authorised person to enter those premises, if necessary by force, at any time within 14 days from the time of the issue of the warrant and search them; and any person who enters the premises under the authority of the warrant may–

(a)   take with him such other persons as appear to him to be necessary;

(b)   seize and remove any documents or other things whatsoever found on the premises which he has reasonable cause to believe may be required as evidence for the purposes of proceedings in respect of such an offence; and

(c)   search or cause to be searched any person found on the premises whom he has reasonable cause to believe to have committed or be about to commit such an offence or to be in possession of any such documents or other things;

but no woman or girl shall be searched except by a woman.'

Comment

4.48   The offences in connection with VAT are contained in s 39; they include broadly speaking, offences of fraudulent evasion of the tax, producing or furnishing a false return with intent to deceive; failures to register for VAT and, of course, failure to pay tax which has been collected from customers and failure to make proper returns. By s 462 of the Criminal Procedure (Scotland) Act 1975, the term 'justice' includes the sheriff and any stipendiary magistrate or justice of the peace.

Style of Application: see Appendix p 147.

(xiv) Weights and Measures Act 1985

Principal object of warrant: entry to premises to inspect equipment and goods or where offence under Act has been, is being or is about to be committed on premises.

Background

4.49 In Scotland every Regional or Island Council has local responsiblity under the Weights and Measures Act 1985 for the administration of the law relating to weights and measures. Under the Act, the council must appoint weights and measures inspectors who carry out day to day enforcement procedures. Under Part II of the Act certain offences are prescribed in connection with weighing or measuring equipment for use for trade; as well as other penalties on conviction, provision is made for forfeiture of equipment.[1] Under Part IV of the Act certain transactions in goods are regulated and other offences are prescribed.[2]

An inspector of weights and measures enjoys certain general powers.

Text of s 79(1) and (2) of the Weights and Measures Act 1985

4.50 Section 79(1) and (2) of the 1985 Act provides:

'(1) Subject to the production if so requested of his credentials, an inspector may, within the area for which he was appointed inspector, at all reasonable times–

(a) inspect and test any weighing or measuring equipment which is, or which he has reasonable cause to believe to be, used for trade or in the possession of any person or upon any premises for such use,

(b) inspect any goods to which any of the provisions of Part IV of this Act or any instrument made under that Part for the time being applies or which he has reasonable cause to believe to be such goods, and

(c) enter any premises at which he has reasonable cause to believe there to be any such equipment or goods, not being premises used only as a private dwelling-house.

(2) Subject to the production if so requested of his credentials, an inspector may at any time within the area for which he was appointed inspector seize and detain–

(a) any article which he has reasonable cause to believe is liable to be forfeited under Part II or IV of this Act, and

(b) any documents or goods which the inspector has reason to believe may be required as evidence in proceedings for an offence under this Act (except an offence under Part V).'

In addition, power to grant a warrant for enforcement purposes is contained in s 79(3)-(6).

Text of s79(3)-(6) of the Weights and Measures Act 1985

4.51   Section 79(3)-(6) of the 1985 Act provides:
'(3) If a justice of the peace, on sworn information in writing–
(a) is satisfied that there is reasonable ground to believe that any
such equipment, goods, articles or documents as are mentioned
in subsection (1) or (2) above are on any premises, or that any
offence under this Act or any instrument made under it (except
an offence under Part V or any instrument made under that Part)
has been, is being or is about to be committed on any premises,
and
(b) is also satisfied either–
(i)   that admission to the premises has been refused, or a refusal
is apprehended, and that notice of the intention to apply for
a warrant has been given to the occupier, or
(ii) that an application for admission, or the giving of such a
notice, would defeat the object of the entry, or that the case
is one of urgency, or that the premises are unoccupied or the
occupier temporarily absent,
the justice may by warrant under his hand, which shall continue in
force for a period of one month, authorise an inspector to enter the
premises, if need be by force.

(4) In the application of subsection (3) above to Scotland, 'justice
of the peace' includes a sheriff.

(5) An inspector entering any premises by virtue of this section
may take with him such other persons and such equipment as may
appear to him necessary.

(6) An inspector who leaves premises which he has entered by
virtue of a warrant under subsection (3) above and which are
unoccupied or from which the occupier is temporarily absent shall
leave the premises as effectively secured against trespassers as he
found them.'

Comment

4.52   The term 'premises' includes any place and any stall, vehicle,
ship or aircraft.[1] It is an offence for any person wilfully to obstruct an
inspector acting in pursuance of the Act;[2] further, any person who,
without reasonable cause fails to give to any inspector acting in
pursuance of the Act any other assistance or information which the
inspector may reasonably require of him for the purpose of the
performance by the inspector of his functions under *inter alia* Pt III
of the Act (which includes section 79(3)) is also guilty of an offence.[3]

Style of Application: see Appendix p 148.

1 Weights and Measures Act 1985, s 94(1)
2 Ibid, s 80
3 Ibid, s 81(1)(b)

(xv) Wireless Telegraphy Act 1949

Principal objects of warrant: entry to premises and search for evidence of offences; examination and test of apparatus found.

Background

4.53 The investigation of wireless telegraphy offences under the Wireless Telegraphy Act 1949 is now carried out by the Department of Trade and Industry Radio Investigation Service. The principal offence prescribed under s 1 of the Act is that of establishing or using any station for wireless telegraphy or installing or using any apparatus for that purpose without a licence issued by the Secretary of State. A full definition of 'wireless telegraphy' is to be found in s 19 of the Act.

Entry and search of premises for enforcement purposes is permitted under warrant granted in terms of s 15(1).

Text of s 15(1) of the Wireless and Telegraphy Act 1949

4.54 Section 15(1) of the 1949 Act provides:

'(1) If, in England, Wales or Northern Ireland, a justice of the peace, or, in Scotland, the sheriff, is satisfied by information on oath that there is reasonable ground for suspecting that an offence under this Act has been or is being committed, and that evidence of the commission of the offence is to be found on any premises specified in the information, or in any vehicle, vessel or aircraft so specified, he may grant a search warrant authorising any person or persons authorised in that behalf by the Secretary of State and named in the warrant, with or without any constables, to enter, at any time within one month from the date of the warrant, the premises specified in the information or, as the case may be, the vehicle, vessel or aircraft so specified and any premises upon which it may be, and to search the premises, or, as the case may be, the vehicle, vessel or aircraft, and to examine and test any apparatus found on the premises, vessel, vehicle or aircraft.'

Comment

4.55 In *Oldfield, Petitioner*[1] it was held that a title to prosecute was not a necessary prerequisite to a title to seek a search warrant. There, a person authorised by the Secretary of State petitioned the sheriff for a warrant even although he could not prosecute in respect of any offence; the sheriff's interlocutor refusing to grant the warrant was recalled by the High Court.

It should be noted that s 15(1) does not confer any power to seize articles found in a search. If it is intended to seize such articles, it is thought that a warrant must be sought at common law by the procurator fiscal.[2]

Style of Application: see Appendix p 149.

1   1988 SCCR 371
2   *Oldfield* does not specifically decide this point, but this was the view of the Crown and seems correct: see 1988 SCCR 371 at 377.

OTHER STATUTORY SEARCH WARRANTS

4.56   The following is merely a list of other statutes containing provision for the granting of warrants to enter premises and/or search them. Only a reference to the individual section is given, with a brief note on the purpose of the warrant and whether information on oath is required. The list is intended to cover the main areas of statutory criminal law not already mentioned, but does not contain references to sections of statutes rarely encountered in practice. Since only basic references are provided here, the reader is strongly advised to consult the full statutory provisions if detailed information is required. The list of statutes is arranged in alphabetical order.

(i)   ARMY ACT 1955 (c 18)
s 186(3) Warrant may be granted by civilian court for arrest of army deserter or person absent without leave. Evidence on oath required that the person is, or is reasonably suspected of being, within the jurisdiction of the court.

(ii)   BETTING GAMING AND LOTTERIES ACT 1963 (c 2)
s 51(1) Sheriff, magistrate or justice of the peace may grant warrant to search premises within jurisdiction in relation to a suspected offence under the Act which is being, has been or is about to be committed on the premises. Information on oath is required.

(iii)   CONSUMER CREDIT ACT 1974 (c 39)
s 162(3) Sheriff, magistrate or justice of the peace may issue warrant to officer of enforcement authority to enter premises to exercise inspection powers or on suspicion that offence has been, is being or is about to be committed on any premises. Evidence on oath required.

(iv) CONTROL OF POLLUTION ACT 1974 (c 40)

s 91(2) Sheriff or justice of the peace may issue warrant to authorised person to enter land or vessel, if need be by force, for the purposes of inspection, measurement, sampling and performing other enforcement functions under the Act. Sworn information in writing required.

(v) COPYRIGHT DESIGNS AND PATENTS ACT 1988 (c 48)

s 109(1) Sheriff or justice of the peace may grant warrant to enter and search premises in connection with certain offences of making or dealing in an article which is an infringing copy of a copyright work, where evidence of offence is in the premises. Application for warrant must be supported by evidence on oath.

s 200(1) Sheriff or justice of the peace may grant warrant to enter and search premises in connection with offences of making, importing or distributing illicit recordings, where evidence of offence is in the premises. Application must be supported by evidence on oath.

(vi) CRIMINAL JUSTICE ACT 1988 (c 33)

s 142(1) Sheriff or justice of the peace may grant warrant to enter and search premises in respect of certain offensive weapons, or offences connected with them; any one of the conditions in s 142(3) must apply. Information on oath not required.

(vii) CRIMINAL PROCEDURE (SCOTLAND) ACT 1975 (c 21)

ss 14, 323 Warrant may be granted by a justice to search for a child against whom specified offence has been or is being committed and to take child to place of safety. Information on oath is required.

s 224 Court making forfeiture order or any justice may grant warrant to search for forfeited articles believed to be on premises, where admission to premises has been refused or refusal is apprehended. Information on oath is required.

(viii) DEER (SCOTLAND) ACT 1959 (c 40)

s 27(2) Sheriff or justice of the peace may grant warrant to search premises, vehicles and boats where evidence of the commission of an offence under the Act is to be found. Persons may also be searched by virtue of such a warrant. Information on oath is required.

(ix) EXTRADITION ACT 1989 (c 33)

s 8 Sheriff has power to grant apprehension warrant in respect of extradition crime; also search warrant in respect of property offence committed in Commonwealth country or colony.

Schedule 1, paras 5, 20 Sheriff or justice of the peace may grant warrant for arrest of fugitive criminal in cases to which Extradition Act 1870 applies.

For detailed procedure, see *Renton and Brown* para 5-45 ff.

(x) FAIR TRADING ACT 1973 (c 37)

s 29(3) Sheriff or magistrate may grant warrant to authorised officer of Weights and Measures Authority to enter premises to exercise inspection powers or on suspicion that offence has been, is being, or is about to be committed on premises. Information on oath required.

(xi) FORGERY AND COUNTERFEITING ACT 1981 (c 45)

s 24(1) Sheriff, stipendiary magistrate or justice of the peace may grant warrant to search premises and seize counterfeits of notes, coins, reproductions and other things used or intended to be used for the making of counterfeits. Information on oath required.

(xii) GAMING ACT 1968 (c 65)

s 43(4) Sheriff, magistrate or justice of the peace may grant warrant to search premises within jurisdiction in connection with offences under the Act. Information on oath is required.

(xiii) INDECENT DISPLAYS (CONTROL) ACT 1981

s 2(3) Sheriff or justice of the peace may grant warrant to constable to enter premises (if need be by force) and to seize article he has reasonable grounds for believing to be or to contain indecent matter and to have been used in the commission of an offence under the Act. Evidence on oath required.

(xiv) OFFICIAL SECRETS ACT 1911 (c 28)

s 9(1) Justice of the peace may grant warrant to search premises for evidence that offence under 1911 Act or Official Secrets Act 1989 has been or is about to be committed. Information on oath required.

(xv) PUBLIC ORDER ACT 1936 (c 6)

s 2(5) Sheriff may grant warrant to search premises for evidence that offence under s 2 has been committed. Offence is (broadly speaking) being involved in the organisation, training, control or management of a quasi-military organisation. Information on oath is required.

(xvi) PUBLIC ORDER ACT 1986 (c 64)

s 24(2) Sheriff or justice of the peace may grant warrant to search premises where it is suspected that material is kept by a person who intends to use it to stir up racial hatred. Reasonable force may be used. Evidence on oath is necessary.

(xvii) SEXUAL OFFENCES (SCOTLAND) ACT 1976 (c 67)
s 18(1)(2) Sheriff, justice of the peace or stipendiary magistrate has power to issue warrant for search and detention of woman or girl unlawfully detained for immoral purposes by any person in any place within his jurisdiction; and also warrant for arrest of any person accused of so unlawfully detaining such woman or girl. Information on oath required.

(xviii) VIDEO RECORDINGS ACT 1984 (c 39)
s 17 Sheriff or justice of the peace may grant warrant to enter and search premises where reasonable grounds exist for suspecting offence under the Act has been or is being committed on the premises, or that evidence of offence may be found there. Evidence on oath required. On the problem of admissibility of evidence of the finding of unclassified videos during a search under warrant, see *Burke v Wilson* 1988 SCCR 361, 1988 SLT 749.

(xix) WILDLIFE AND COUNTRYSIDE ACT 1981 (c 69)
s 19(3) Sheriff or justice of the peace may grant warrant to enter and search premises for the purpose of obtaining evidence that offences under the Act have been committed. Information on oath is required.

WARRANTS ISSUED BY SECRETARY OF STATE

4.57 A small number of statutes provide for the granting of a warrant by the executive, rather than the judiciary. These exceptional statutes recognise, to a limited extent, a doctrine of State necessity which is quite at odds with the general law on the inviolability of private property and personal liberty. In certain restricted cases, Parliament has given power under statute to the Secretary of State for Scotland or officials under his authority to grant warrants authorising certain acts, without the necessity of any judicial scrutiny at the time the warrant is issued. Two such statutes required brief mention here.

Interception of Communications Act 1985

4.58 Section 1(1) of the Interception of Communications Act 1985 makes it an offence for a person intentionally to intercept a communication in the course of its transmission by post or by means of a public telecommunication. But this is subject to an exception where the communication is intercepted in obedience to a warrant issued by the Secretary of State under s 2. By s 2(1) such a warrant may require the person to whom it is addressed to intercept, in the course of their transmission by post or by means of a public telecommunications system, such communications as are described in the warrant, which may also require the disclosure of the information so obtained to such persons and in such manner as are described in the warrant.

Such warrants cannot be issued unless the Secretary of State considers that the warrant is necessary:

(a) in the interest of national security;
(b) for the purpose of preventing or detecting serious crime; or
(c) for the purpose of safeguarding the economic wellbeing of the United Kingdom.[1]

There are extensive provisions in the Act covering the scope of such warrants;[2] their issue and duration;[3] the means by which such warrants may be modified;[4] and the safeguards which must be applied.[5] A Tribunal is established to whom a person aggrieved by the interception of a communication to or by him may apply for an investigation[6] and a Commissioner is appointed to keep under review the functions of the Secretary of State and to assist the tribunal; the Commissioner makes an annual report to Parliament.[7]

It must be noted that while the 1985 Act makes it an offence to put a 'tap' on a telephone without a warrant, the practice of 'telephone tapping' has to be distinguished from 'tracing' a telephone call to the extent of discovering the telephone number from or to which the call was made: such tracing operations do not require any warrant and they are not criminal when they are made for the prevention or detection of crime or for the purposes of any criminal proceedings.[8]

1 Interception of Communications Act 1985, s 2(2)
2 Ibid, s 3
3 Ibid, s 4
4 Ibid, s 5
5 Ibid, s 6
6 Ibid, s 7
7 Ibid, s 8. In his report for 1990 the Commissioner (the Rt Hon Lord Justice Lloyd) revealed that the Secretary of State for Scotland authorised sixty-six warrants for telephone taps in that year, an increase of three on 1989. Most of the warrants concerned the importation and distribution of drugs: see *The Glasgow Herald* 15 June 1991.
8 Telecommunications Act 1984, s 45 (as substituted by s 11 and Sch 2 of the Interception of Communications Act 1985).

Security Service Act 1989

4.59 Until the passing of the Security Service Act 1989, the

Security Service (MI5) was not recognised in law and its officers had no executive powers to arrest or search. Likewise there was no machinery for dealing with complaints by people claiming or believing that they had been subject to action by the Service, something which probably breached the European Convention of Human Rights. Following the judgement of the European Court in *Leander v Sweden*[1] and a number of revelations by former officers of the Service as to how it operated, a legal framework was devised which set out (sometimes only in generality) what the Service was entitled to do and how its actions might be kept under review. Two statutory functions of the Service are laid out in s 1(2) and (3) of the 1989 Act: firstly, the protection of national security and, in particular, its protection against threats from espionage, terrorism and sabotage, from the activities of agents of foreign powers and from actions intended to overthrow or undermine parliamentary democracy by political, industrial or violent means; and secondly, to safeguard the economic well-being of the United Kingdom against threats posed by the actions or intentions of persons outside the British Islands.

The operations of the Service are under the control of its Director General, who is responsible for its efficiency and whose duty it is to ensure

'that there are arrangements for securing that no information is obtained by the Service except so far as necessary for proper discharge of its functions or disclosed by it except so far as necessary for that purpose or for the purpose of preventing or detecting serious crime'.[2]

1   (1987) 9 EHRR 433
2   Security Service Act 1989, s 2(2)(a)

4.60   If it be thought that the statutory functions of the Service are extremely extensive, loosely described and capable of many interpretations which might imperil personal liberty, the provisions of the Act which govern the granting of warrants are subject to the same criticisms. Section 3(1) provides that no entry on or interference with property shall be unlawful if it is authorised by a warrant issued by the Secretary of State under this section. It is thereafter provided:

'The Secretary of State may on an application made by the Service issue a warrant under this section authorising the taking of such action as is specified in the warrant in respect of any property so specified, if the Secretary of State:

(a) thinks it necessary for the action to be taken in order to obtain information which

    (i) is likely to be of substantial value in assisting the Service to

discharge any of its functions;
(ii) cannot reasonably be obtained by other means; and
(b) is satisfied that satisfactory arrangements are in force under s
2(2)(a) above with respect to the disclosure of information
obtained by virtue of this section and the information obtained
under the warrant will be subject to those arrangements.'[1]

It will immediately be observed that the power to issue the warrant is not subject to any of the tests set out in other statutes authorising the issuing of a warrant by a court. The Secretary of State does not have to be satisfied on information given to him that there is reasonable ground for suspecting that the action which the Security Service wish to take is justified and relates to its functions. While he must think it 'necessary' he does not appear to be obliged to follow any recognised legal route in coming to his decision. Nor is there any apparent requirement that the information sought to be obtained under the warrant relates to any suspected or alleged crime.

Such a warrant can only be granted by the Secretary of State personally or, in any urgent case where the Secretary of State has expressly authorised its issue and a statement of that fact is endorsed on it, under the hand of an official of his department of or above Grade 3.[2] A warrant under the hand of the Secretary of State personally lasts for six months, while those under the hand of his officials expire at the end of the period ending with the second working day following the day of grant.[3] Provision is made for extension by six months of the period of initial validity.[4] A warrant may also be cancelled by the Secretary of State if he is satisfied that the action authorised by it is no longer necessary.[5]

1 Security Service Act 1989, s 3(2)
2 Ibid, s 3(3)
3 Ibid, s 3(4)
4 Ibid, s 3(5)
5 Ibid, s 3(6)

4.61 Provision is also made under the Act for the appointment of a Commissioner[1] and a Tribunal[2] with similar functions to those appointed under the Interception of Communications Act 1985, on which the provisions of the 1989 Act are based. Only by such means can the aggrieved citizen have the propriety of warrant by the Secretary of State brought under review.

1 Security Service Act 1989, s 4
2 Ibid, s 5

5. The admissibility of evidence obtained under a search warrant

INTRODUCTION

5.01 Since the whole purpose of a search warrant is to obtain evidence which may subsequently be used in criminal proceedings, the admissibility of that evidence is an issue which inevitably arises in every case. The fruits of a search may be many and varied, but quantity and type are not the criteria for determining the essential evidential question. It has already been observed that the reasons for granting a warrant which is *ex facie* valid are usually of little interest to the court trying a case where a specific criminal offence is alleged and such reasons will often be irrelevant to the issue of guilt or innocence.[1] But when there is tendered in evidence a verbal account of what was done under the warrant, accompanied by the production of items recovered, then the court may be faced with an objection to the admissibility of the evidence. Such an objection may be taken on many different grounds, such as that the warrant was defective in form; that the required statutory procedures were not carried out; that they were not completed; that the search was not confined within the terms of the warrant or that it strayed beyond its bounds; or that the items recovered did not actually relate to the enquiry. The objection will of course require to be argued and decided before the case can be determined and the decision will often have a profound effect on the course of the proceedings.[2] Even if the objection is, on the face of it, a good one, the court may nonetheless be entitled to hold that any defect in form or procedure is excusable, or to hold that such a situation of urgency existed at the time the warrant was executed that any irregularity ought to be excused in the wider interests of justice.[3]

1 See *supra* para 1.10.
2 In summary cases the evidence may have to be heard under reservation of all questions of competency and relevancy and the issue determined at the end of the Crown case: see eg *Burke v Wilson* 1988 SCCR 361, where the proceedings before the sheriff are narrated at 362-365. In cases taken on indictment, any objection may have to be determined outwith the presence of the jury.
3 See *infra* paras 5.11–5.13.

5.02 By their decisions on such matters, the courts indirectly control the activities of the police and set the limits of acceptable activity within the parameters of any warrant previously granted. Thus, essential legal principles are identified, refined and developed by the judges in a way well recognised and typical of the Scottish method of legal reasoning. It is significant in this regard that it was the High Court, and not Parliament, which set out the considerations to be applied in deciding the admissibility or otherwise of evidence obtained by illegal or irregular means. The case of *Lawrie v Muir*[1] is so well known that it is probably otiose to refer to it again, but the famous *dicta* of Lord Justice-General Cooper do bear repeating on the question of resolving the competing interests involved. He observed:

'From the standpoint of principle it seems to me that the law must strive to reconcile two highly important interests which are liable to come into conflict - (a) the interest of the citizen to be protected from illegal or irregular invasions of his liberties by the authorities, and (b) the interest of the State to secure that evidence bearing upon the commission of crime and necessary to enable justice to be done shall not be withheld from Courts of law on any merely formal or technical ground. Neither of these objects can be insisted upon to the uttermost. The protection of the citizen is primarily protection for the innocent citizen against unwarranted, wrongful and perhaps high-handed interference, and the common sanction is an action of damages. The protection is not intended as a protection for the guilty citizen against the efforts of the public prosecutor to vindicate the law. On the other hand, the interest of the State cannot be magnified to the point of causing all the safeguards for the protection of the citizen to vanish, and of offering a positive inducement to the authorities to proceed by irregular methods.'[2]

These *dicta* are equally apt to cover the situation of evidence obtained by means of an improper warrant (or in excess of the powers thereunder) as they are to cover that of other evidence acquired by improper means, such as where the police have extracted a confession from a suspect by virtue of an unfair interrogation. The law of warrants is equally unproductive of an absolute rule, with the result that each situation has to be considered on its own facts before a decision can be taken on whether the irregularity is fundamental and fatal to the admissibility of the evidence. This makes it difficult to state the law with the certainty which might be considered essential when questions such as the liberty of the subject and the protection of his proprietary interests are involved, and against the background of the relative articles of the European Convention on Human Rights.[3] But such a consideration fails to recognise a phenomenon often referred to as the natural flexibility of the common law of

Scotland, a concept which in the context of criminal law is frequently lauded, preened and invoked by the High Court.[4]

1   1950 JC 19.
2   Ibid at 26 - 27.
3   For a discussion of the European Convention, see Ewing and Finnie, *Civil Liberties in Scotland* (2nd edn), ch 2.
4   See eg Memorandum by Lord Justice-General Cooper to the Royal Commission on Capital Punishment, Minutes of Evidence, p 428; *Khaliq v HM Advocate* 1984 SLT 137; *McKay v HM Advocate* 1991 SCCR 364.

5.03   The area of discretion to admit evidence can, once entered, assume an amorphous quality. Each step taken to execute a warrant can be scrutinised in detail; the effects upon the person whose premises are searched can be assessed in the light of his knowledge (if any) of what is going on; and the interests of State versus individual can be weighed in the balance. All that can be said with some certainty is that a flaw in form or procedure may imperil the search, although not of course until the results are later scrutinised in court. As Lord Cooper observed further in *Lawrie v Muir*[1]:

'Irregularities require to be excused, and infringements of the formalities of the law in relation to these matters are not lightly to be condoned. Whether any given irregularity ought to be excused depends upon the nature of the irregularity and the circumstances under which it was committed. In particular, the case may bring into play the discretionary principle of fairness to the accused which has been developed so fully in our law in relation to the admission in evidence of confessions or admissions of a person suspected or charged with crime. That principle would obviously require consideration in any case in which the departure from the strict procedure had been adopted deliberately with a view to securing the admission of evidence obtained by an unfair trick. Again, there are many statutory offences in relation to which Parliament has prescribed in detail in the interests of fairness a special procedure to be followed in obtaining evidence, and in such cases (of which the Sale of Food and Drugs Act provides one example) it is very easy to see why a departure from the strict rules has often been held to be fatal to the prosecution's case. On the other hand, to take an extreme instance figured in argument, it would usually be wrong to exclude some highly incriminating production in a murder trial merely because it was found by a police officer in the course of a search authorised for a different purpose or before a proper warrant had been obtained.[2]

What follows is an account of how the law of Scotland has tried to reconcile the opposing interests in resolving the dilemma of admissibility.

1   1950 JC 19.
2   Ibid at 26 - 27.

REGULAR SEARCHES

5.04   Little need be said about the admissibility of evidence of what was done and what was found during a regular search under warrant. Assuming the warrant is not too wide, that there are no irregularities in the form of warrant or in its execution, and provided the terms of the warrant were not exceeded, then articles found will normally be admissible in evidence. As a matter of good practice, such items are lodged as productions and spoken to in evidence, although there are of course many situations where production is impractical and is unnecessary anyway for the proof of the Crown case.[1] Admission of evidence of the fruits of a regular search under warrant necessarily implies that there is met the test of relevance to the case being tried.[2]

1   See *Renton and Brown* para 18-04 and the cases there cited.
2   On admissibility of such evidence generally, see *Stair Encyclopaedia of the Laws of Scotland*, vol 10, paras 690-700.

IRREGULAR SEARCHES

Warrant too wide

5.05   In former times it seems that a general warrant to search for stolen goods was illegal. Hume regarded as exceptionable a warrant 'to make search everywhere' for such goods.[1] But Alison qualifies this somewhat:

'The search warrant must be special as to the goods intended to be searched for, or at least the felony which it is intended to elucidate, and bring to punishment by the warrant craved for; but it does not appear to be indispensable that it should set forth the particular house meant to be searched for these goods, anymore than the particular place where the criminal is suspected to be concealed. It seems in short to be a sufficient authority to search for the goods specified, taken on the felonious occasion charged, everywhere, in the same manner as it is sufficient warrant to search for the individual suspected whenever he is to be found.'[2]

Whatever the position as to unrestricted searches at the beginning of the nineteenth century, it later became tolerably clear that a warrant to search premises had to be specific as to the purpose and limitations of the search. In *Webster v Bethune*[3] the court suspended a wide general warrant to search for stolen articles where the petition on which it was granted contained no indication as to the time when, or the person by whom the articles were said to have been stolen. Nor was there any specification in the warrant itself of the premises which might be searched thereunder. In *Bell v Black and Morrison*[4] the application proceeded upon averments of a suspected conspiracy in connection with which written documents and other articles were said to be in the possession of certain persons. Warrant was granted to search for these documents without any real restriction as to the particular documents concerned, a proceeding which was later struck down on the basis that it would have permitted the seizure of the whole papers of each person, whether they inculpated him or not. Strong disapproval of the warrant was also expressed in subsequent civil litigation arising from its execution, although the absence of adequate security against oppressive use appears to have weighed heavily with some judges.[5]

It follows from this that an application in the nature of a 'fishing diligence' is likely to be strongly resisted. A recent example of a wide and indefinite warrant being suspended by the High Court was *British Broadcasting Corporation v Jessop*.[6] In that case, police were investigating a potential breach of s 2 of the now-repealed Official Secrets Act 1911 wherein the BBC in Glasgow were said to be in possession of highly classified information in connection with preparation of a series of programmes entitled 'The Secret Society'. A warrant was obtained authorising a named officer of Strathclyde Police

'to enter said premises occupied by the British Broadcasting Corporation at Queen Margaret Drive, Glasgow and if necessary to use force for making such entry whether by breaking open doors or otherwise and to search said premises and if necessary every person found therein and to seize any sketch, plan, model, article, note or document or anything of a like nature including in particular any film which is evidence of an offence under said Act having been or being about to be committed which he may find on said premises or on any such person and with regard to or in connection with which he has reasonable ground for suspecting that an offence under said Act has been or is about to be committed and for that purpose to make patent all shut and lockfast places in said premises ...'.

This warrant was successfully attacked on the basis that it contained no specification of what offence had been or was about to be committed or to what section of the 1911 Act any such offence related. Interim suspension was granted (while the search was actually going on); a later application was made for a proper warrant, which was granted.[7]

1 *Hume* II, 78.
2 Alison *Practice*, 146, 147.
3 (1857) 2 Irv 597.

4   (1865) 5 Irv 57; (1865) 3 M 1026
5   *Nelson v Black and Morrison*; (1866) 4 M 328.
6   High Court of Justiciary, Edinburgh, February 1987, *unreported.*
7   See *The Scotsman*, 2 February, 1987.

Irregularities in form: 'excusable defects'

5.06   The whole question of formalities of a warrant has already been considered.[1] It will be remembered that certain formalities eg signature, are essential and their absence will render the warrant void, with the consequence that evidence of what was done under the warrant and the fruits of any search will normally be inadmissible. Other formalities, though desirable, are not absolutely essential, and their absence may be excused. It is this latter class of case which can give rise to difficulties in the law of evidence, for solutions depend on individual circumstances.

The act of applying the principles set out in *Lawrie v Muir*[2] by balancing the opposing interests of the state and the accused may have the result that defects in a warrant can be regarded as of little moment. In such cases the evidence of what was done under the warrant may well be admitted. In *Allan v Milne*[3] a warrant under the Misuse of Drugs Act 1971 was obtained to search for drugs in the premises occupied by 'Paul Ashbourne and others' at 178 Leith Walk, Edinburgh. Only when the police arrived to execute the warrant did they discover that there was no 'Paul Ashbourne' there, but a Phyllis Ashburn, her sister Marion Ashburn and two other persons. A search was nonetheless carried out but nothing was found. Some days later a further search was carried out under the authority of the same warrant by a different officer who did not know that the designation of the occupiers in the warrant was incorrect. This search revealed the presence of controlled drugs; although evidence of the search was objected to, it was admitted on the basis that the irregularity was not such as would render the warrant unlawful. In any event, the sheriff held that any irregularity was excusable and had not resulted in unfairness to the accused. In *HM Advocate v Strachan*,[4] a warrant which was properly signed but which omitted the sheriff's name and designation was held not to be invalid and evidence of the search carried out thereunder was admitted.

It is thus a question of circumstances as to whether a defect can be excused. Obviously, the more serious the crime under investigation, the more important will be the public interest element in the necessary balancing exercise. Likewise, a major (but not fatal) blunder in the terms of the warrant may make it more difficult to exercise discretion in favour of admitting the evidence, while a minor typographical error may be easy to excuse. It is important to remember that in deciding whether to cure a defect in a warrant, a court does so indirectly, by deciding whether to admit evidence of what was done under the defective warrant rather than by conducting an inquiry as to how the defect arose and discovering what was allegedly the true position. For example, it is incompetent to lead evidence as to the date of a warrant where the date is missing or incomplete.[5]

1 See *supra*, para 1.10 ff.
2 1950 JC 19.
3 1974 SLT (Notes) 76.
4 1990 SCCR. 341. But see *HM Advocate v Cumming* 1983 SCCR 15 where certain errors of form in a drugs warrant were held not to be excusable. On statutory warrants under the 1971 Act, see *supra* paras 4.24-4.26.
5 See eg *Bulloch v HM Advocate* 1980 SLT (Notes) 5; *HM Advocate v Welsh* 1987 SCCR 647.

Irregularities in execution

5.07 Before considering cases where the police or other officers executing a warrant have gone beyond the terms of the warrant itself, it is necessary to pause and look briefly at the situation where in carrying out the authorised actings, the officers have done so in an irregular manner. Suppose for example, the warrant authorises the search of a dwellinghouse at 123 Main Street, Anytown for the proceeds of a housebreaking alleged to have occurred the previous day at 456 Back Street. Do the officers have any discretion as to how the search is carried out? Are the police entitled to attend in great numbers to execute the warrant? Must they do so without causing maximum disturbance not only to the occupants but to those who may live nearby? Scots law provides no clear answers to such questions in the absence of specific provision in the warrant; in any event they raise serious issues of personal liberty, some of which are addressed elsewhere in this book, particularly in relation to the use of force.[1] How the police carry out their duties is a matter not just of law, but of efficient policing in the public interest, with a view to the prevention and detection of crime in the interests of all. Oppressive police behaviour is objectionable (as is all oppression) but the dividing line between oppression and good detective work is not always easy to draw. Oppression is a claim often made, and not just by those who are innocent; such an allegation is not easily answered by a claim of 'the greater public good' when a full scale police raid takes place in the middle of the night, complete with support services in case of trouble. The problem in this field is deciding just what is 'regular' or 'reasonable', something on which the case law in Scotland is noticeably silent. A warrant may entitle the police to 'turn over' the contents of a house, but it never instructs the police to turn the contents back after extracting any items for which the search is being conducted.[2]

From the standpoint of admissibility of evidence, such problems probably only arise where it is alleged that evidence has been obtained as a result of unfair behaviour on the part of the police. But, as will be seen, those cases which have arisen deal mostly with urgent situations where evidence may be lost, or with 'the fruit of the forbidden tree', where suspicious articles outwith the terms of the warrant are found and proffered in evidence.[3] The latter situation is particularly vexing where a search has been carried out under warrant, but the warrant itself is not produced at the trial. In *Nocher v Smith*[4] it was argued that such non-production was fatal to the admissibility of the evidence of what was recovered in the search, on the basis that it was impossible for the defence to ascertain whether there was any irregularity in the warrant, and if so its nature, and the circumstances in which the irregularity was committed. This objection was repelled by the sheriff; a subsequent appeal against conviction failed, the High Court holding that in the circumstances any irregularity was excusable since the police had carried out the proper procedure in good faith. But there appears to be no case where it has been specifically held that because of unfair or oppressive conduct on the part of the police in executing a valid warrant *within its terms*, the evidence of what was found is inadmissible.

1 See *supra* para 1.22 ff.
2 Cf the position in England under Code B made under the provisions of the Police and Criminal Evidence Act 1984, where specific provisions are made as to the conduct of searches.
3 See *infra* para 5.09 ff.
4 1978 SLT (Notes) 32.

Actings in excess of warrant

5.08 A random or speculative search deliberately carried out under the cover of a specific search warrant is illegal.[1] It is necessary to keep within the terms of the warrant; and if those purporting to execute it do not know what it contains, they will be held to have executed an illegal search. In *Leckie v Miln*,[2] the accused appeared on petition on a charge of theft of a wallet and a purse allegedly taken from particular premises. On his first appearance, the normal warrant was granted to search the person, repositories and domicile of the accused, for items tending to establish guilt or participation in the crime. In fact, two officers ignorant of the charge and not even in possession of the warrant went to the accused's home following information from a colleague that the accused had been arrested. At the house they told the accused's co-habitee of the accused's arrest on a petition warrant and asked for permission to search the house. This permission was given; in the course of the search the police found items later said to have been stolen from an office and a school. The accused later stood trial on charges of theft from the latter places, when evidence was admitted as to the items found in his house on the basis that his co-habitee had impliedly given her consent to the search. On appeal against conviction, it was held that the search actually carried out was neither authorised by the warrant nor by any implied consent of the co-habitee, since any consent given by her must be assumed to have been given on the basis that the officers were acting within the warrant, which was limited to a search in respect of the crime charged. The High Court thus quashed the convictions on the basis that the search had been random and unauthorised, and that the articles recovered had been inadmissible in evidence.

The case was clearly complicated by the absence of knowledge on the part of the police of what they were searching for; that made the search a speculative exercise.[3] But that will not be so where the police have the necessary knowledge. Nor will the search be illegal if the place where the search is to be conducted is clearly specified and there are no other defects in form or procedure. In *Guthrie v Hamilton*[4] a drugs warrant authorised the search of '45 Church Street, Inverkeithing' and any person found therein. As the warrant was being executed, an individual knocked on the door of that house. The police opened it and found him standing on the doorstep. As he entered he was detained, searched and found to be in possession of cannabis. At his trial it was objected that the search of his person was illegal, since he was not on the premises but only on the doorstep. The sheriff repelled the objection and admitted evidence of the finding of the cannabis. On appeal against conviction the High Court held that since the premises named in the warrant had to include not merely the house itself but also the garden ground, the path leading to the front door and certainly the doorstep itself, the accused was clearly a person who was found in the premises at that time and the search was therefore authorised by the warrant.

But the real difficulty in this area is where the police know the terms of the warrant (even if they do not have it with them), actively search for the items mentioned therein at the place authorised but find something else suspicious but not covered by the warrant. Are they to shut their eyes to such items? To answer this, courts sometimes apply another test.

1 Good or bad faith on the part of the party responsible for an irregularity is an important element in deciding whether to excuse any irregularity in the obtaining of evidence: *Fairley v Fishmongers of London* 1951 JC 14 at 24. See also *McAvoy v Jessop* 1988 SCCR 172.
2 1982 SLT 177.
3 For a comment on this case, see Finnie 'Police Powers of Search in the Light of *Leckie v Miln*' 1982 SLT (News) 289.
4 1988 SCCR 330, 1988 SLT 823. See also *McCarron v Allan* 1988 SCCR 9.

THE 'HEPPER' PRINCIPLE

5.09 It often happens in practice that police officers lawfully carrying out a search under a proper warrant for specific goods mentioned are left in a state of uncertainty as to the evidential value of other items which they may uncover in the course of the search. Natural suspicion might tend them to the view that, for example, expensive stereo equipment in the house of a young person in receipt only of income support may not have been lawfully acquired, a suspicion which is unlikely to be removed by a requirement of dogged adherence to a warrant authorising only a search for controlled drugs. In law, an active search for stereo equipment is illegal under a drugs warrant, but evidence of the finding of the stereo may nonetheless be admitted. This proposition flows from two well known cases which are sometimes hard to reconcile. In *HM Advocate v Turnbull*[1] the police had been investigating the affairs of an accountant. They obtained a warrant to search his premises for evidence of fraudulent income tax returns made on behalf of a particular client. But when the police carried out the search, they uplifted also a large number of files relating to other clients and each marked with the name of the client to which it related. Another warrant was obtained six months later, under cover of which the Crown later argued that the fruits of the extended search should be admitted. This argument was rejected; the court refused to admit evidence of articles not found in conformity with the original warrant. While it was not argued that the initial retention of all the files was *per se* illegal, (it being conceded that they had to be examined to discover whether they did in fact relate to the first warrant) once it became clear that they did not bear upon the affairs of the original client, they could not be used to enable subsequent charges to be brought home. In particular, possession and use of the documents was not obtained under the second warrant, which authorised only the future and not past actions of officers of law. This was not a situation where the police had come accidentally upon evidence of a plainly incriminating character; the nature of the evidence only became apparent later, and there were no circumstances of urgency. By contrast *HM Advocate v Hepper*[2] concerned a search not under warrant, but with consent of the occupier of the house to be searched. The search was in connection with a particular matter, but in the course of the search the police found a briefcase which was unrelated to the purpose of the search but which turned out to have been stolen. At the accused's trial on the charge of theft of the case, the evidence as to its finding was held to be admissible on the basis that the case was of a very suspicious character (since it contained the name and address of another person) and that it had been 'stumbled upon' by the police. The police action was characterised as entirely proper: Lord Guthrie observed that if the case had not been taken away by them, it might have disappeared. And even if their action was irregular, the interests of society in the detection of crime justified its removal.[3]

In the light of these two cases, the law has been summarised to the following effect: once the police are lawfully on premises with a search warrant they may take away any suspicious articles they happen to see, but cannot actively search for articles outwith the warrant or take away articles which might on further examination disclose further offences.[4] This of course makes it somewhat problematic for all parties. From the viewpoint of the suspect, his right to have the integrity of his household protected against illegal searches has to be balanced against the interest of society in detecting and prosecuting crime. From the viewpoint of the police, the dividing line between an 'active' search and a 'passive' stumble may not always be easy to identify, for example, in the house of a resetter which turns out to be the proverbial Aladdin's cave. And from the viewpoint of the court, the evidential decision will usually have a dramatic effect, one way or another, on the progress of the case which is finally brought to trial.

1   1951 JC 96; 1951 SLT 409.
2   1958 JC 39.
3   Ibid at 40.
4   See *Renton and Brown* para 5-40 and cases there cited. For another application of the Hepper principle, see *Burke v Wilson* 1988 SCCR 361, 1988 SLT 749.

5.10   Two recent cases illustrate the problems. The *Hepper* principle was applied in *Tierney v Allan*,[1] where police had searched a house on a warrant referring to stolen gas cylinders. One of the officers looked beneath a cot in the course of a general search of a room and saw a typewriter; his colleague recognised it as similar to some typewriters he knew were the subject of a reported theft. The typewriter was taken as a production and the householder charged *inter alia* with its reset. At the trial, the sheriff admitted the evidence as to the finding of the typewriter after hearing evidence that the first officer did not expect to find it under the cot. On appeal against conviction, it was held that the search was lawful; during it an officer had come across the typewriter in a strange place unexpectedly (it being clearly visible at a glance); and that as there had been no deliberate search beneath the cot, the evidence had been rightly admitted. In particular there was no question of a random search.

But a somewhat different result was reached in *Innes v Jessop*.[2] There, a warrant had been granted under the Firearms Act 1968, the object of the search being firearms and ammunition. In the course of the search the police found *inter alia* a driving licence and a sub-contractors' tax exemption certificate which were lying among other items in the householder's bedroom. The police also removed a number of other articles which were totally unconnected with firearms. The householder was convicted of reset of the licence and the certificate, evidence having been admitted as to the circumstances in which these items were found. On appeal, it was held that the removal of the other articles carried an implication that the search was random and the conviction could not be sustained. This was not a case of the unexpected discovery of an article which aroused suspicion during the course of a lawful search for the material covered by the warrant.

These contrasting cases show that the whole circumstances of the search will be examined in cases where objection is taken to the admissibility of evidence of articles found; it is reasonably clear that if there is any hint of unfairness, trickery or even over-zealous police practice, then the evidence may not be admitted. But there is yet another category of case where irregularities or failures may be overlooked in the wider interests of justice: the controversial subject of "urgency" now requires examination.

1   1989 SCCR 344.
2   1989 SCCR 441.

SITUATIONS OF URGENCY

5.11 The concept of urgency has, from time to time, been invoked to provide a vehicle for excusing the lack of proper procedure in carrying out searches and for justifying the admission in evidence of the articles found. The idea that the urgent demands of the situation could be relied on for these purposes has been developed mainly in the context of searches without warrant, but has spilled over occasionally into situations where a search warrant has been granted but because of some irregularity in form or procedure, the warrant cannot be relied upon as a solid legal foundation for a search. A good example of a case where no warrant was obtained is *McHugh v HM Advocate*[1] where an accused was charged with assault and robbery. Shortly after the alleged crime the police learned that some numbered bank-notes had recently been in the possession of two men, believed to be the accused and a co-accused. Both were arrested; thereafter the police searched the house and person of the accused. This search was said to be with his consent and after charge. On his person, the police found certain numbered bank-notes and coins. The trial judge admitted the evidence of the search, despite objections on the basis that the arrest was of questionable legality. Following conviction, the High Court on appeal held that in the circumstances the evidence supported the view that the search was lawful and in any event it was essential as a matter of urgency. The risk was of course that any numbered bank-notes which the accused had in his possession might be lost or destroyed, and from that point of view the search was justified, on the general principle that the interests of justice should not be thwarted by insistence that the proper formalities should be gone through.

While in *McHugh* and other similar cases (notably *Bell v Hogg*[2]) the urgency is the supposed justification for not obtaining a warrant, it is clear that urgency may justify departure from the normal rules even where a warrant is extant. As was observed by Lord Justice-General Cooper in *Lawrie v Muir*,[3] there is no absolute rule; it is all a question of circumstances, but clearly something more than just administrative convenience in carrying out proper procedure is required. Even serious inconvenience, on its own, is unlikely to be enough; the various factors relevant to the admissibility of evidence irregularly obtained require to be assessed, and urgency is but one of these.[4]

1   1978 JC 12.
2   1967 JC 16.
3   1950 JC 19 at 26, 27.
4   It may indeed be sufficient without further enquiry. In *Bell v Hogg* 1967 JC 49, urgency was said not merely to excuse but to justify an irregularity in the obtaining of evidence. See 1967 JC 49 at 56, 59, 61.

5.12   Urgency was invoked in *HM Advocate v McKay*,[1] a case where an Irish warrant had been issued to search premises in Dublin for cash suspected to have come from a safeblowing incident in a bank in Glasgow. Goods recovered during the search included money and certain documents. Objection was taken by the defence to the admissibility of any documents recovered which were not documents in the name of the accused, but these were admitted at the subsequent trial. The court took the view that even if the warrant was exceeded (something which was doubtful even if Scottish procedure was invoked), the observations of Lord Cooper in *Lawrie v Muir* were apt to cover the situation; the evidence was not necessarily inadmissible just because of any irregularity; and in any event there were circumstances of urgency which rendered it appropriate to admit the evidence. The same result was reached in *Walsh v MacPhail*,[2] where an invalid search warrant could not be relied on. The accused was a serviceman at an RAF base who was suspected of keeping controlled drugs in his room. Unknown to him, a sniffer dog had been used to identify the area of the base in which the drugs were thought to be located, which area included the accused's sleeping quarters. His room was sealed; he was then summoned by an officer and asked for his consent to the room being searched. Following his refusal of consent, a purported warrant was granted by a senior officer authorising a search which was subsequently carried out and which revealed the presence of drugs in the room. At the accused's trial for possession of cannabis it was conceded that the warrant was invalid, in that it had not been granted by a person empowered to do so under the Misuse of Drugs Act 1971, but the sheriff admitted the evidence of the fruits of the search, which was essential in support of the Crown case. On appeal against conviction, the High Court upheld the sheriff's view that the urgency of the situation justified the action being taken, on the basis that there was no-one on the base who was entitled to obtain a proper warrant under the 1971 Act and that had it been necessary to use the procedures under the Act it was possible that the drugs which were eventually found in the room might have been removed and disposed of. The Court rejected any suggestion that the actions of the investigators amounted to an unfair trick; on the contrary, they were held to have acted in good faith.

This decision has been criticised on the basis firstly that any risk of destruction of the evidence in the circumstances was more imaginary than real, due to the restrictions on movement which military discipline imposed; and secondly, that the base was not situated in so remote a part of Scotland that the obtaining of a proper warrant would have been unduly onerous.[3] Such criticisms are, it is thought, equally apt to cover the suggestion in *Hay v HM Advocate*[4] that the urgency of the situation might have justified the admission of the evidence of the accused's dental impressions, even if the warrant there had been improperly granted.[5] It will be remembered that Hay was an inmate of an approved school at the time he was

suspected of the murder; he was not the master of his own movements and had already voluntarily given two impressions of his teeth
before the warrant was applied for. In such a situation the authorities
(who knew he was a suspect) were hardly likely to permit him to visit
the dentist and risk the loss of evidence, the very fear which the High
Court expressed as an argument for invoking the 'urgency' justification. Perhaps this issue was not explored in *Hay* as fully as it merited,
no doubt because the real issue of whether the warrant was competent was resolved in favour of the Crown.

1   1961 JC 47.
2   1978 SLT (Notes) 29.
3   See Finnie, 'Police Powers of Search in the Light of *Leckie v Miln*' 1982 SLT
    (News) 289 at 291, 292.
4   1968 JC 40.
5   Ibid at 48.

5.13   One recent case where urgency appears to have been relied on
is *MacNeil v HM Advocate*.[1] A number of accused were charged with
importation or being concerned in the importation of cannabis,
contrary to the Customs and Excise Management Act 1979. Following discovery of a large amount of cannabis on a vessel in a Scottish
harbour, customs officers searched the home in Liverpool of one of
the accused by virtue of writ of assistance. Certain articles were
removed which were not liable to forfeiture under the Act. At the
subsequent trial an objection was taken to evidence about these items
on the basis that they had been irregularly obtained. This objection
was repelled; the trial judge held that the officers had not acted
irregularly and that in any event any irregularity was excusable in
view of the urgency of the situation. This reasoning was upheld on
appeal; the articles in question were described as being manifestly of
evidential value in relation to the very serious offence of which the
accused was suspected. At the time the search was carried out,
customs officials throughout the United Kingdom were dealing with
a 'fluid and developing' situation which had become one of considerable urgency. In particular, it was liable to result in the disappear-
ance or loss of evidence unless proper steps were taken to prevent
that. The necessity of seizing the articles was 'clamant'. It was held
that in the circumstances of a very important investigation into grave
charges, the interests of the public in the due administration of justice
heavily outweighed the interests of the accused as an individual.

Quite apart from considerations of urgency, the trial judge in
MacNeil described the case as being nearer to those such as *HM
Advocate v Hepper*[2] rather than the line of cases in which *HM Advocate
v Turnbull*[3] was the starting point. This was clearly correct; indeed,

he adopted the reasoning in *HM Advocate v McKay*[4] on the question of whether the search exceeded the warrant; it might not have been beyond the authority of the warrant to take possession of articles pointing to the whereabouts of other items liable to forfeiture under the 1979 Act.

In *Burke v Wilson*,[5] urgency was said to justify the removal of certain obscene video tapes which the police discovered during a search under warrant for unclassified videos in respect of which an offence under s 10 of the Video Recordings Act 1984 was being committed; evidence was admitted on the Hepper principle as to what was found on the basis that the police had accidentally stumbled upon the tapes which were of a very suspicious character and which might have disappeared had the police not removed them.

Urgency, then, is all a question of circumstances, which like so many elements on the law of admissibility, makes it hard to state the law with any certainty. But by not fettering the discretion of a court dealing with such an issue, it is easy to claim that the most satisfactory method of reconciling the various competing interests is thus achieved.

1   1986 SCCR 288.
2   1958 JC 39.
3   1951 JC 96, 1951 SLT 409.
4   1961 JC 47.
5   1988 SCCR 361, 1988 SLT 749 (per the Lord Justice-Clerk and Lord Wylie at 752, 753; Lord Dunpark decided the case on other grounds.)

CONCLUSION

5.14   The flexibility of Scots law to deal with changing circumstances is vividly illustrated by the cases examined in the foregoing paragraphs. Indeed they are clear examples of a legal system operating on the basis of principle rather than precedent, and without recourse to rigid rules contained either in statute, code of practice or line of authority.[1] But this approach, while much vaunted, is said to have drawbacks other than just the uncertainty of what the law is at any given time.

The first of these drawbacks is the alleged inconsistency between operating alongside each other a rule that real evidence obtained by illegal means may be admitted and a rule that a confession obtained by illegal, or at least unfair means, will be excluded. This inconsistency, highlighted by Sheriff Macphail,[2] deserves somewhat closer scrutiny than has been previously afforded to it, especially in connection with the law of warrants. As is evident from all the material previously discussed, a warrant is sought precisely for the purpose of obtaining the authority of the court for a particular course of action which impinges on the civil liberty of the subject. If the warrant is defective in some non-essential particular, or is formally valid, executed properly but exceeded by the seizing of suspicious material not expressly covered by it, it is equally as easy to argue that the evidence obtained ought to be admitted in the absence of unfairness or trickery, as it is to argue that a confession obtained in circumstances which disclose no unfairness should likewise be admitted. A confession extracted by unfair means which place 'cross examination, pressure and deception in close company'[3] is no more likely to be admitted in evidence than the fruits of a search carried out in bad faith in circumstances of trickery and in order to flout the law. In this area, it is suggested that good faith on the part of the police and fairness to all parties are the most important of all the factors which have to be assessed in deciding whether to admit evidence otherwise irregularly obtained, especially in those cases where a warrant is in fact granted but the actings thereunder are challenged in some way.[4]

Another supposed drawback of not operating strictly defined rules is said to be that the police will be encouraged to 'chance their arms'. To this it may be replied that there will always be police officers whose perception of duty is less than proper, whether their failings are simply to be overzealous, grossly reckless or just plain criminal. It is precisely because the liberty of the individual is involved that the law requires the interposing of an independent judicial officer between the policeman and the private citizen. The consideration of an application for a warrant is not, or should not be, taken lightly. The signature of the judge is not a formality; he requires to be vigilant at all times in conformity with his judicial oath. Once he has granted the warrant, the individual magistrate has no practical control in most cases over how the police execute the warrant, although he would probably be justified in law in attending personally with the police to ensure that his warrant was in fact carried out in terms.[5] Of course that is never done in practice; courts nowadays control the actions of police indirectly and at a later stage by their decisions on the admissibility of evidence. The actual presence of a magistrate during a drugs raid would no doubt be an appalling prospect, in operational terms, for any self-respecting divisional police commander. But the element of secondary control does in practice seem to work well; there appears to be no great impetus for change.

The final criticism which is sometimes made of the absence in Scots law of any strict exclusionary rule in this field is that notions of fairness vary from judge to judge, and from a wider viewpoint, from time to time. So far as the former is concerned, whether evidence is admitted or excluded may depend on the outlook of the trial judge; while any mistakes he makes could be corrected by the appeal court, the latter's findings would only be of relevance to the accused if he were the appellant; errors in favour of the defence resulting in exclusion of evidence and ultimate acquittal could only be scrutinised on a Lord Advocate's Reference.[6] Consistent views of fairness may thus be difficult to regulate. This is not just the case at any one period of the law's development. Nothing is clearer from the authorities that notions of fairness and fair dealing change with the age.[7] Perhaps this is not quite as marked in relation to real evidence irregularly obtained as it is in relation to confessions in the same category, but there has undoubtedly been a move away from applying 'academic vetoes' which ignore practical reality. This move has gone hand in hand with a general desire not to exclude any relevant evidence and to allow juries or other arbiters of fact to assess its credibility, reliability and weight. That of itself inevitably leads to great inconsistency, for appeal courts are extremely reluctant to enter the area of factual dispute; once a wrong decision on fact is made, it is often incapable of correction in a manner which demonstrates a consistent approach.

To all this, it may be replied: it was always thus, and always will be. No fact finding process can ever be perfect and no set of rules can ever be immutable. The law on warrants is no different in this respect from any other branch of criminal jurisprudence.

1 Cf the position in England and Wales under the Police and Criminal Evidence Act 1984 and the relative Codes of Practice thereunder.
2 Macphail *Evidence* (1987) para 21-06.
3 See *Jones v Milne* 1975 JC 16.
4 On good and bad faith as an element in the decision whether to excuse irregularities, see *Stair Memorial Encyclopaedia*, vol 10 para 697 and the cases there cited.
5 In *Nelson v Black and Morrison* (1866) 4 M 328 at 332 it was observed that the presence of the Sheriff to superintend the search carried out was necessary to prevent oppression and that the illegality of the warrant lay in the absence of such a security.
6 See Criminal Procedure (Scotland) Act 1975, s 263A.
7 Contrast eg in the law of confessions, the cases of *HM Advocate v Rigg* 1946 JC 1 and *Hartley v HM Advocate* 1979 SLT 26.

Appendix of styles

The following appendix contains an assorted selection of applications for warrants encountered in practice. In addition to the statutory applications specifically discussed in Part 4 of the book, a number of other styles are included. The standard form of warrant has already been described at para 1.04 and it is adapted in common practice if necessary to meet any specialities which arise in individual cases.

Any collection of legal styles must be a matter of personal preference and those found herein are no exception.

LIST OF STYLES

(a) Common Law Applications
  (i) Application for search warrant: proceeds of housebreaking
  (ii) Application for search warrant: clothing
  (iii) Application for warrant to take sample
  (iv) Application for warrant for internal examination
  (v) Application for warrant to search bank premises
  (vi) Application for warrant to take teeth impressions
  (vii) Application for warrant to apprehend for purpose of photographing and fingerprinting.
  (viii) Application for warrant to apprehend absconding witness.
(b) Applications under particular statutes
  (i) Bankers' Books Evidence Act 1879, s 7
  (ii) Criminal Justice (Scotland) Act 1987, s 50(4)
  (iii) Criminal Justice (Scotland) Act 1987, s 39
  (iv) Criminal Justice (Scotland) Act 1987, s 52(4)
  (v) Explosives Act 1875, s 73
  (vi) Firearms Act 1968, s 46(1)
  (vii) Food Safety Act 1990, s 32(2)

123

    (viii) Misuse of Drugs Act 1971, s 23(3)

    (ix) Prevention of Terrorism (Temporary Provisions) Act 1989, s 15(1)

    (x) Salmon and Freshwater Fisheries (Protection) (Scotland) Act 1951, s 11(1)

    (xi) Taxes Management Act 1970, s 20c

    (xii) Trade Descriptions Act 1968, s 28(3)

    (xiii) Value Added Tax Act 1983, Sch 7 para 10(3)

    (xiv) Weights and Measures Act 1985, s 79(3)

    (xv) Wireless Telegraphy Act 1949, s 15(1)

(a) COMMON LAW APPLICATIONS

(i) PROCEEDS OF HOUSEBREAKING

UNDER THE CRIMINAL PROCEDURE (SCOTLAND)
ACT 1975
IN THE SHERIFF COURT OF
THE PETITION OF THE REGIONAL PROCURATOR
FISCAL

HUMBLY SHEWETH:

That from information received by the Petitioner, it appears that on
at
said premises were broken into/forced open and
were stolen therefrom and there are reasonable grounds for believing
that the stolen property or part thereof is in the house/premises at

occupied by

The Petitioner therefore craves the Court to grant Warrant to
or other Officers of Law to
enter said house/premises occupied by
and if necessary to use force for making such entry, whether by
breaking open doors or otherwise and to search the said house/
premises and to secure and take possession of any articles which such
Officers have reason to believe are part of the proceeds of such theft
and for that purpose to make patent all shut and lockfast places in
said house/premises or to do further or otherwise as to your Lordship
shall seem meet.

ACCORDING TO JUSTICE

Procurator Fiscal Depute

(ii) APPLICATION FOR SEARCH WARRANT: CLOTHING

UNDER THE CRIMINAL PROCEDURE (SCOTLAND)
ACT 1975
IN THE SHERIFF COURT OF
THE PETITION OF THE REGIONAL PROCURATOR
FISCAL

HUMBLY SHEWETH:

That from information received by the Petitioner, it appears that

It further appears that there are reasonable grounds for believing that
which may have been worn by the Perpe-
trator may be in the house at
occupied by
and that it is desirable in the public interest that the house at
be searched by Officers of Police to secure
any evidence that may be therein.

The Petitioner therefore craves the Court to take the Oath of
to the effect aforesaid and there-
after to grant Warrant authorising him with such assistance as he may
find necessary to enter the house at
and if necessary to use force for
making such entry, whether by breaking open doors or otherwise,
and to search the said premises and to secure and take possession of
any of the forementioned articles which he has reason to believe are
pertinent to the investigation of said crime and for that purpose to
make patent all shut and lockfast places in said premises, or to do
further or otherwise as to your Lordship may seem meet.

ACCORDING TO JUSTICE

Procurator Fiscal Depute

(iii) SAMPLE TO BE TAKEN

UNDER THE CRIMINAL PROCEDURE (SCOTLAND)
ACT 1975
IN THE SHERIFF COURT OF
THE PETITION OF THE REGIONAL PROCURATOR
FISCAL

HUMBLY SHEWETH:

(1) That on   ,
appeared on Petition at   Sheriff Court charged with

(2) That on said date said
was committed for further examination/until liberated in due course
of law and was ordered to be detained in custody.

(3)

(4) That it is necessary in the interests of justice that a sample of
            be taken from the said   .

May it therefore please your Lordship to grant Warrant to Officers
of Strathclyde Police to convey said
from   to
for the purpose of taking said sample and to grant Warrant to
                                        to take said
sample of   from the said   .

ACCORDING TO JUSTICE

Procurator Fiscal Depute

(iv) INTERNAL EXAMINATION

UNDER THE CRIMINAL PROCEDURE (SCOTLAND)
ACT 1975
IN THE SHERIFF COURT OF
THE PETITION OF
PROCURATOR FISCAL OF COURT FOR THE PUBLIC
INTEREST

[*Place*] [*Date*]

HUMBLY SHEWETH:

That on   ,   ,
was detained in   by police officers under the
terms of the Misuse of Drugs Act 1971; that the said
is detained under Section 23(2) of said Act on suspicion of being in
possession of a controlled drug in contravention of said Act or of
regulations made thereunder;

That there are reasonable grounds to suspect that the said
has controlled drugs within his
person and a medical examination is therefore required.

The Petitioner therefore craves the Court to take the oath of
, Drug Squad, Police Head-
quarters   to the effect aforesaid
and thereafter to grant warrant to officers of law to convey the said
to
there to be examined for the presence of controlled drugs within his
person, by medical practitioners and by a radiologist if it appears
necessary and by such means to said practitioners to be reasonable,
including Proctoscopy and Gastroscopy and X-ray examination to
regain and to take possession of any such substances thereof and to
make swabs of such substances as seems necessary.

ACCORDING TO JUSTICE

Procurator Fiscal Depute

(v) SEARCH OF BANK PREMISES

UNDER THE CRIMINAL PROCEDURE (SCOTLAND)
ACT 1975
IN THE SHERIFF COURT OF
THE PETITION OF
PROCURATOR FISCAL

HUMBLY SHEWETH:

1. On   , a cheque for   was issued by
District Council Housing Department and had
been presented at   Bank Plc at
and credited to an account there on

2. A complaint has been made by
that said cheque had been stolen and had been drawn and uttered as
aforesaid without his authority.

3. It is believed that the holder of said account is
but officials at said Bank decline to advise the Police of the address
of the holder of the account to which said cheque was credited
without a judicial order.

4. The Petitioner therefore is of necessity applying to your Lordship
for a warrant to search said Bank, to examine records held there to
discover the address of the holder of the account to which said
cheque was credited.

The Petitioner therefore craves the Court to grant warrant to
Constable   of
Police and other Officers of Law, authorising them, with such
assistance as they may find necessary, to enter and search said
premises occupied by said   Bank Plc at
forrecords
and for that purpose to make patent all shut and lockfast places in
said premises and to examine said records and seize same if necessary.

ACCORDING TO JUSTICE

Procurator Fiscal Depute

(vi) TEETH IMPRESSIONS

UNDER THE CRIMINAL PROCEDURE (SCOTLAND)
ACT 1975
IN THE SHERIFF COURT OF
THE PETITION OF THE REGIONAL PROCURATOR
FISCAL

HUMBLY SHEWETH:

1. That on   ,   was assaulted at
                                    and that as a result of said assault was
found to have been bitten;

2. That said   's injuries were subsequently
photographed by a member of   Police Identification
Bureau;

3. That said   's injuries and the photographs thereof
were examined by Doctor at the   Dental Hospital
and that said Doctor has identified some of said injuries as human
bites;

4. That said Doctor is of the view that there is sufficient detail in the
human bites to allow identification of the person who inflicted them;

5. That the person alleged to have assaulted said as specified in
paragraph 1 hereof is born and residing at

6. That it is desirable in the public interest that impressions,
photographs and measurements be taken of the teeth of said
                    for comparison with the injuries specified at
paragraph 3 hereof.

May it please your Lordship to grant warrant (a) to Officer of
                    Police, or other officers of   Police to
convey said to the   Dental Hospital for said impressions,
photographs and measurements to be obtained; and (b) to said
Doctor and such other Doctors in the   Dental Hospital
as he may consider appropriate, to examine the teeth of said and
obtain casts thereof.

ACCORDING TO JUSTICE

Procurator Fiscal Depute

(vii) PHOTOGRAPHING AND FINGERPRINTING

UNDER THE CRIMINAL PROCEDURE (SCOTLAND)
ACT 1975
IN THE SHERIFF COURT OF
THE PETITION OF THE REGIONAL PROCURATOR
FISCAL

HUMBLY SHEWETH:

That prior to appearing on Petition   was
required by Officer of   Police, to attend at
                    Police Office, in answer to a Petition Warrant
previously granted in respect of   in order that he be
photographed and that samples of his fingerprints be obtained; that
said   failed to report to said
                    Police Office and was not photographed and
said fingerprint samples were not taken; that said
                                    has thereafter been given an
opportunity to report to said   but
has failed to do so; that it appears to the Petitioner that it is necessary
in the interests of justice and for the furtherance of the investigation
into said charge that said   be
photographed and said fingerprint samples be taken from him.

The petitioner therefore craves the court to grant warrant to aforesaid
and other officers of   Police to apprehend the said
                    , to convey him to said Police
Office, to photograph said and obtain said fingerprint samples from
him.

ACCORDING TO JUSTICE

Procurator Fiscal Depute

(viii) ABSCONDING WITNESS

UNDER THE CRIMINAL PROCEDURE (SCOTLAND)
ACT 1975
IN THE SHERIFF COURT OF
THE PETITION OF THE REGIONAL PROCURATOR
FISCAL

HUMBLY SHEWETH:

That   is a material witness for the Crown
(in an Indictment at the instance of Her Majesty's Advocate,) against
for the Crown charging him with

That the said   has absconded from his
address at
aforesaid, without leaving any information as to where he may be
found.

That from the information available to the Petitioner he has good
cause to believe that the said   has
absconded to avoid being cited to giving evidence at the trial of said
Indictment which is due to be tried at a sitting of the High Court of
Justiciary, within the Criminal Courthouse,
commencing on   .

May it therefore please your Lordship to examine on Oath,
of Strathclyde Police, as to the
facts averred, and to grant warrant to Officers of Law to search for
and apprehend the said   and
bring him before you for examination in the premises, and thereafter
to commit him to the Prison of   , therein to be
detained until the trial of the said
or until the said   finds sufficient
caution for his compearance at the said trial to bear witness as
aforesaid.

ACCORDING TO JUSTICE

Procurator Fiscal Depute

(b) APPLICATIONS UNDER PARTICULAR STATUTES

(i) BANKERS' BOOKS EVIDENCE ACT 1879, s 7

SHERIFF COURT OF
THE PETITION OF
PROCURATOR FISCAL OF COURT FOR THE PUBLIC
INTEREST

HUMBLY SHEWETH:

That on   , appeared in Your Lordships Court on a
complaint at the instance of the Petitioner charging said
                              with fraud. A copy of said complaint is
attached and referred to for its terms.

That from information received by the Petitioner, it appears that
evidence relative to said charges may be obtained from bank account
number   in the name of said
                   Bank Plc at

That the Petitioner is under the necessity of inspecting and obtaining
copies of entries in the Bankers' Books of said Bank relative to said
accounts.

The Petitioner therefore craves the Court to grant an Order that the
Petitioner be at liberty, with such assistance of Officers of Law as may
be necessary, to inspect and take copies of any entries in said Bankers'
Books for the purposes aforesaid, and to serve a copy of said order on
said Bank, all in terms of the Bankers' Books Evidence Act 1879,
Section 7.

ACCORDING TO JUSTICE

Procurator Fiscal Depute

(ii) CRIMINAL JUSTICE (SCOTLAND) ACT 1987, s 50(4)

UNDER THE CRIMINAL PROCEDURE (SCOTLAND)
ACT 1975 SECTION 50
SHERIFFDOM OF
THE PETITION OF THE REGIONAL PROCURATOR
FISCAL FOR THE PUBLIC INTEREST

HUMBLY SHEWETH:

That at Glasgow Airport on   at   hours
                              residing at
was detained by Officers of HM Customs and Excise.

That said Officers have reasonable grounds for suspecting that said
                              had committed or was committing a
relevant offence as defined in the Criminal Justice (Scotland) Act
1987, Section 50 (11).

That said Officers have reasonable grounds for suspecting that in
connection with the commission of such an offence a controlled drug
is secreted in the body of said

That said   is presently detained at the
Customs Office at Glasgow Airport, Paisley under the powers
contained in Section 50(1) and (3) of said Act and that the period of
detention so authorised expires at   hours on   , the
officer aftermentioned continues to have reasonable grounds for
suspecting (i) that said   has committed or
is committing a relevant offence and (ii) that a controlled drug is
secreted in the body of said

That it is necessary in the public interests that said
                              be further detained for the purposes
specified in Section 50(2) of said Act.

The petitioner therefore craves the Court to take the Oath or
Affirmation of   a superior Officer of
Customs and Excise to the effect foresaid and thereafter to grant a
Warrant in terms of Section 50(4) of said Act for the further

detention of said   at said Customs Office
for an additional period of 7 days commencing at   hours on
                    .

                                        In respect whereof

                                        Procurator Fiscal

(iii) CRIMINAL JUSTICE (SCOTLAND) ACT 1987, s 39

UNDER THE CRIMINAL PROCEDURE (SCOTLAND)
ACT 1975
IN THE SHERIFF COURT OF
THE PETITION OF THE REGIONAL PROCURATOR
FISCAL

HUMBLY SHEWETH:

(1) That there are reasonable grounds for suspecting that
has carried on or has derived financial or
other rewards from drug trafficking and the Petitioner has a duty to
investigate the same.

(2) That   is believed to be in possession
of material relevant to said drug trafficking namely:

(3) That there are reasonable grounds for suspecting that said
material:–

(i) is likely to be of substantial value (by itself or together with
other material) to said investigation;
(ii) does not consist of or include items subject to legal
privilege.

(4) That there are reasonable grounds for believing that it is in the
public interest, having regard:–
(a) to the benefit likely to accrue to said investigation if said material
is obtained;
(b) to the circumstances under which said
in possession of said material holds the same;

(5) That access to said material should be given and it would not be
appropriate to make an order in terms of Section 38 of the Criminal
Justice (Scotland) Act 1987 in relation to said material because

The Petitioner therefore craves the Court in terms of Section
39(2)(b) of said Act to grant Warrant authorising
with such assistance as he may find
necessary to enter the said premises occupied by
at

and if necessary to use force for making such entry, whether by breaking open doors or otherwise and to search the said premises for said material and in terms of Section 39(5) of said Act to seize and retain said material other than items subject to legal privilege which is likely to be of substantial value (whether by itself or together with other material) to this investigation and for that purpose to make patent all shut and lockfast places in said premises or to do further or otherwise as to your Lordship may seem meet.

ACCORDING TO JUSTICE

Procurator Fiscal Depute

(iv) CRIMINAL JUSTICE (SCOTLAND) ACT 1987, s 52(4)

UNDER THE CRIMINAL PROCEDURE (SCOTLAND)
ACT 1975
IN THE SHERIFF COURT OF
THE PETITION OF THE REGIONAL PROCURATOR
FISCAL

HUMBLY SHEWETH:

That from credible information which the Petitioner has received on
            at
the following offence was committed, namely
and that said offence may involve serious or complex fraud in respect
of which a direction as to its investigation was issued by Her Majesty's
Advocate on   , all in terms of section 51 of the Criminal
Justice (Scotland) Act 1987;

That   is the nominated officer entitled to
exercise the powers and functions conferred by sections 52 to 54 of
said Act in respect of said investigation;

That   has by notice in writing dated
            required   to produce on
at
to the said   the following documents which appear to relate to matters relevant to said investigation;

That there are reasonable grounds for believing that the said
                                has failed to produce the said documents
as aforesaid and that they are on the premises at

Therefore the Petitioner craves the court to grant warrant to
                                to enter (using such force as is reasonably
necessary for the purpose) the said premises at

, to search them and to take possession of
and to take in relation to them any other steps which may appear to
be necessary for preserving them and preventing interference with
them, all in terms of section 52(4) of said Act.

ACCORDING TO JUSTICE

Procurator Fiscal Depute

(v) EXPLOSIVES ACT 1875, s 73

UNDER THE CRIMINAL PROCEDURE (SCOTLAND)
ACT 1975
IN THE SHERIFF COURT OF
THE PETITION OF THE REGIONAL PROCURATOR
FISCAL

HUMBLY SHEWETH:

That from information received by the Petitioner, there is reasonable
cause to believe that an offence has been or is being committed with
respect to an explosive in
or that an explosive is in such place in contravention of the Explosives
Act 1875 and the Explosive Substances Act 1883.

The Petitioner therefore craves the Court to take the Oath of
of Strathclyde Police to the effect
foregoing and thereafter to grant Special Warrant authorising said
with such assistance as he may find
necessary to enter such place and every part thereof and if need be
by force and search same and every person found therein for
explosives and to seize and detain any explosives which may be found
in such place all in terms of the Explosives Act 1875, Section 73 and
the Explosive Substances Act 1883, Section 8.

ACCORDING TO JUSTICE

Procurator Fiscal Depute

(vi) FIREARMS ACT 1968, s 46(1)

UNDER THE CRIMINAL PROCEDURE (SCOTLAND)
ACT 1975
IN THE SHERIFF COURT OF
THE PETITION OF THE REGIONAL PROCURATOR
FISCAL

HUMBLY SHEWETH:

That from information received by the Petitioner, there are reasonable grounds for suspecting that an offence relevant for the purposes of Section 46 of the Firearms Act 1968 and the Firearms Act 1982 has been, is being, or is about to be committed in the premises occupied by
in contravention of said Acts.

The Petitioner therefore craves the Court to take the Oath of of Strathclyde Police to the effect foregoing and thereafter to grant Warrant authorising him with such assistance as he may find necessary, to enter said premises if necessary by force and to search the said premises and every person therein and to seize and detain any firearm as defined by the aforementioned Acts, or ammunition which he may find on the said premises or any person therein, in respect of which or in connection with which he has reasonable grounds for suspecting that an offence relevant for the purposes of the aforesaid Section 46 of the Firearms Act 1968 and the aforesaid Firearms Act 1982 has been, is being or is about to be committed, all in terms of the Firearms Act 1968, Section 46.

ACCORDING TO JUSTICE

Procurator Fiscal Depute

(vii) FOOD SAFETY ACT 1990, s 32(2)

UNDER THE CRIMINAL PROCEDURE (SCOTLAND)
ACT 1975
IN THE SHERIFF COURT OF
THE PETITION OF THE REGIONAL PROCURATOR
FISCAL

HUMBLY SHEWETH:

That from information received by the Petitioner, it appears that
                              is an authorised Officer of a local
Authority, namely   District Council
Environmental Health Department, having in terms of and subject
to the provisions of Section 32(1) of the Food Safety Act 1990 a right
to enter upon premises at all reasonable hours for the purpose of
ascertaining whether there is or has been on the premises any
contravention of the provisions of said Act or of any regulations made
thereunder being provisions which said Authority are required or
enjoined to enforce and generally for the purpose of the performance
by said authority of their functions under said Act or such regulations.

That said   wishes for such purposes to
enter premises, namely
and there are reasonable grounds for entry into such premises for
such purposes but an application for admission or the giving of notice
of intention to apply for a Warrant would defeat the object of the
entry.

The Petitioner therefore craves the Court to take the Oath of said
                              to the effect foregoing and thereafter to
grant Warrant to said authorised Officer to enter said premises, if
need by force, taking with him such other persons as may be
necessary, such Warrant to continue in force for a period of one
month, all in terms of the Food Safety Act 1990, Section 32(2).

ACCORDING TO JUSTICE

Procurator Fiscal Depute

(viii) MISUSE OF DRUGS ACT 1971, s 23(3)

UNDER THE MISUSE OF DRUGS ACT 1971
IN THE SHERIFF COURT OF
THE PETITION OF THE REGIONAL PROCURATOR
FISCAL

HUMBLY SHEWETH:

That from credible information received by the Petitioner, there is reasonable ground for suspecting (a) that controlled drugs as specified in Schedule 2 of the Misuse of Drugs Act 1971, as amended, are in contravention of said Act or Regulations made thereunder, in the possession of a person on the premises at

occupied by   and/or (b) that a document as specified in Section 23(3)(b) of said Act is in the possession of a person, on the premises at
occupied by

The Petitioner therefore craves the Court to take the oath of   of   Strathclyde Police to the effect foresaid and to grant warrant, in terms of Section 23(3) of said Act, authorising him or any other Officer of Strathclyde Police at any time or times within one month from the date of said warrant, if granted, to enter, if need be by force, the premises specified and to search said premises and any persons found thereon and if there is reasonable ground for suspecting that an offence under said Act has been committed in relation of any said controlled drugs found on said premises or in the possession of any such persons, or that any document so found is such a document as is mentioned in Section 23(3)(b) of said Act, to seize and detain those drugs or that document, as the case may be.

ACCORDING TO JUSTICE

Procurator Fiscal Depute

(ix) PREVENTION OF TERRORISM (TEMPORARY PROVISIONS) ACT 1989, s 15(1)

UNDER THE CRIMINAL PROCEDURE (SCOTLAND)
ACT 1975
IN THE SHERIFF COURT OF
THE PETITION OF THE REGIONAL PROCURATOR
FISCAL

HUMBLY SHEWETH:

That from information received by the Petitioner, there are reasonable grounds for suspecting that   is or has been concerned in the commission, preparation or instigation of acts of terrorism within the meaning of the Prevention of Terrorism (Temporary Provisions) Act 1989, that he is liable to arrest under section 14(1)(b) thereof and that he is to be found on the premises at
occupied by   .

The Petitioner therefore craves the Court to take the oath of   of   Police to the effect foregoing and thereafter to grant warrant to   with such assistance as he may find necessary to enter, by force if necessary, the said premises for the purpose of searching for and arresting the said all in terms of Section 15(1) of said Act.

ACCORDING TO JUSTICE

Procurator Fiscal Depute

(x) SALMON AND FRESHWATER FISHERIES (PROTECTION) (SCOTLAND) ACT 1951, s 11(1)

UNDER THE CRIMINAL PROCEDURE (SCOTLAND)
ACT 1975
IN THE SHERIFF COURT OF
THE PETITION OF THE REGIONAL PROCURATOR
FISCAL

HUMBLY SHEWETH:

That from information received by the Petitioner there are reasonable grounds for suspecting that an offence under Section   of the Salmon and Freshwater Fisheries (Protection) (Scotland) Act 1951 has been committed and that evidence of the offence may be found on the premises occupied by   at

The Petitioner therefore craves the Court to take the oath of
                    of   Police to the
effect foregoing and thereafter to grant warrant to said
                         with such assistance as he may find necessary at any time or times within one week of the date hereof to enter, if necessary by force, upon said premises, to search them and every person who is found thereon, all for the purpose of detecting said offence, all in terms of Section 11(1) and (2) of said Act.

ACCORDING TO JUSTICE

Procurator Fiscal Depute

(xi) TAXES MANAGEMENT ACT 1970, s 20(c)

UNDER THE TAXES MANAGEMENT ACT 1970
IN THE SHERIFF COURT OF
THE PETITION OF
AN OFFICER OF THE BOARD
WITHIN THE MEANING OF THE TAXES
MANAGEMENT ACT 1970
ACTING WITH THE APPROVAL OF SUCH BOARD IN
RELATION TO THIS PARTICULAR CASE

HUMBLY SHEWETH:

That there is reasonable ground for suspecting that an offence involving serious fraud in connection with, or in relation to, tax is being, has been or is about to be committed in respect of the affairs of   and that evidence of it is to be found on premises, namely

The Petitioner therefore craves the Court to take the Oath of   to the effect foregoing and thereafter to issue a Warrant authorising him to enter said premises if necessary by force, at any time within fourteen days from the issue of said Warrant, to search them and to seize and remove any things whatsoever found there which he has reasonable cause to believe may be required as evidence for the purposes of proceedings in respect of such an offence, all in terms of the Taxes Management Act 1970, Section 20c.

ACCORDING TO JUSTICE

Petitioner

(xii) TRADE DESCRIPTIONS ACT 1968, s 28(3)

UNDER THE CRIMINAL PROCEDURE (SCOTLAND) ACT 1975
IN THE SHERIFF COURT OF
THE PETITION OF THE REGIONAL PROCURATOR FISCAL

HUMBLY SHEWETH:

That from information received by the Petitioner, it appears that there is reasonable ground to believe that an offence under the Trade Descriptions Act 1968 has been, is being or is about to be committed on premises, namely
and that an application for admission, or the giving of a notice of intention to apply for a Warrant under Section 28(3) of said Act would defeat the object of the entry.

The Petitioner therefore craves the Court to take the Oath of   a duly authorised Officer of a local Weights and Measures Authority, namely,
Regional Council, Consumer and Trading Standards Department to the effect foregoing and thereafter to grant Warrant authorising him with such other persons and equipment as may appear to him necessary to enter at any time within one month of the date of said Warrant said premises at
by force if need be, for the purpose of the execution of his powers under Section 28 of said Act, all in terms of Section 28(3) of said Act.

ACCORDING TO JUSTICE

Procurator Fiscal Depute

(xiii) VALUE ADDED TAX ACT 1983 Schedule 7 para 10(3)

UNDER THE VALUE ADDED TAX ACT 1983
IN THE SHERIFF COURT OF
THE PETITION OF
AN OFFICER OF CUSTOMS AND EXCISE
AND AN AUTHORISED PERSON FOR THE PURPOSES
OF THE VALUE ADDED TAX ACT 1983

HUMBLY SHEWETH:

That there is reasonable ground for suspecting that an offence in connection with Value Added Tax is being, has been, or is about to be committed in the premises occupied by
at
and that evidence of the commission of such an offence is to be found at the premises aforesaid.

The Petitioner therefore craves the Court to take the Oath of said
to the effect foregoing and thereafter to
issue a Warrant authorising said   together
with such other persons as appear to him to be necessary to enter said premises within fourteen days from issue of said Warrant if necessary by force, to search them and to seize and remove any documents or other things whatsoever found there which he has reasonable cause to believe may be required as evidence for the purpose of proceedings in respect of an offence in connection with Value Added Tax and to search or cause to be searched any person found on the said premises whom he has reasonable cause to believe to have committed or to be about to commit such an offence or to be in possession of any documents or other things as above mentioned, all in terms of the Value Added Tax Act 1983, Section 38 and Schedule 7, Paragraph 10(3).

ACCORDING TO JUSTICE

Petitioner

(xiv) WEIGHTS AND MEASURES ACT 1985, s 79(3)

UNDER THE CRIMINAL PROCEDURE (SCOTLAND)
ACT 1975
IN THE SHERIFF COURT OF
THE PETITION OF THE REGIONAL PROCURATOR
FISCAL

HUMBLY SHEWETH:

That from information received by the Petitioner, it appears that there is reasonable ground to believe that an offence under the Weights and Measures Act 1985 or any instrument made thereunder, has been, is being or is about to be committed on premises, namely
and that an application for admission, or the giving of a Notice of Intention to apply for a Warrant under said Act would defeat the object of the entry.

The Petitioner therefore craves the Court to take the Oath of
an Inspector of Weights and Measures
of a local Weights and Measures Authority, namely,
Regional Council, Consumer and Trading Standards Department, to the effect foregoing and thereafter to grant Warrant authorising him with such other persons and equipment as may appear to him necessary to enter at any time within one month of the date of said Warrant said premises at
by force if need be, for the purpose of the execution of his powers under Section 79 of said Act, all in terms of Section 79(3) of said Act.

ACCORDING TO JUSTICE

Procurator Fiscal Depute

(xv) WIRELESS TELEGRAPHY ACT 1949, s 15(1)

UNDER THE CRIMINAL PROCEDURE (SCOTLAND)
ACT 1975
IN THE SHERIFF COURT OF
THE PETITION OF THE REGIONAL PROCURATOR
FISCAL

HUMBLY SHEWETH:

That there is reasonable ground for suspecting that an offence under the Wireless Telegraphy Act 1949, Section 1(1) (other than one consisting in the installation or use, otherwise than under and in accordance with a wireless telegraphy licence, of any apparatus not designed or adapted for emission (as opposed to reception)) is being/ has been committed in the premises at
in the Sheriffdom of   and that evidence of the commission of the offence is to be found in the said premises and that it is necessary for the Petitioner to apply to the court for a Warrant under Section 15(1) of the Wireless Telegraphy Act 1949 as amended by the Telecommunications Act 1984.

The Petitioner therefore craves the Court to take the Oath of
Officer of the Radio Investigation Service, Department of Trade and Industry, to the effect foresaid and thereafter to grant a Warrant under the said Section authorising said
and   being persons authorised in that behalf by the Secretary of State with or without any Constables to enter at any time within one month from the date of the Warrant the premises specified in the Petition and (1) to search the said premises and examine and test any apparatus found there and (2) seize and detain any apparatus or other thing found there which appears to the said
and   to have been used in connection with or to be evidence of the commission of such offence.

ACCORDING TO JUSTICE

Procurator Fiscal Depute

Index

Reference to text are by paragraph number;
references to appendix are by page numbers

151